Using the
Track Record
Approach

Using the Track Record Approach

The Key to Successful Personnel Selection

Charles A. Dailey

amacom

A DIVISION OF AMERICAN MANAGEMENT ASSOCIATIONS

The author gratefully acknowledges the encouragement he received from Robert Andrews, William Buel, Richard Nachman, Robert Pearse, and Martin Peeler. Without their professional interest this book would not have been possible.

Library of Congress Cataloging in Publication Data

Dailey, Charles Alvin.
  Using the track record approach.

  Bibliography: p.
  Includes index.
  1. Employee selection.   I. Title.
HF5549.5.S38D34   658.3'112   81-69371
ISBN 0-8144-5695-2   AACR2

First Printing

Contents

1

Why a New Personnel Selection System Now?

How productive people are hired and identified as promotable is our problem—not a new problem, but newly urgent. Among the reasons for urgency are legal pressures and—above all—the crisis in American productivity. If you need an example of the first, people over 35 now constitute almost a majority of the U.S. workforce. That is a large number of people, and they are not likely to be hesitant about litigation to ensure or increase their job rights.

In multinational firms and corporations in other countries, there may be no exact equivalent of the Equal Employment Opportunity (EEO) law, but in most instances the political pressures on hiring and promotion are as great as in the United States, or greater.

The productivity challenge is really a challenge to human resources planners to produce something that unfortunately is rare: innovation in personnel procedures. Can this innovation be found in the methods by which we identify talent? Several very promising new trends in the behavioral sciences provide reasons for optimism.

This is fortunate, since these trends bring us fresh ideas just as the traditional assessment methods (for hiring and promotion) have seemingly lost their ability to solve our problems or even to capture our imagination.

1

The Decline of Traditional Assessment Methods

Under the legal and other pressures of the times, every selection procedure has shown its flaws. These legal pressures, however, are much broader than the scope of EEO legislation itself. They flow from the demands of an increasingly better educated and sophisticated workforce. The demands particularly include certain rights that will be outlined in early chapters. For example, everyone wants to know how he or she will be judged, by whom, and on what grounds.

It *is* possible to design an assessment system that grants and even advances the job candidate's rights; and it is *not* necessary that the employer lose rights in order to grant them to the employee. In this book, we will assume that the rights of the employer and of the job candidate are as follows:

Candidate's Rights	*Employer's Rights*
To be judged by those who are competent in judging.	To expect initiatives from the candidate to facilitate the process of judging the candidate.
To be assessed by substantive methods rather than by trivia.	To evaluate the candidate more thoroughly if the position imposes greater risk to the employer.

The following paragraphs briefly discuss the status of the principal traditional assessment methods, particularly as they relate to the rights of job candidates in the selection process.

The Decline of Testing. The use of standardized tests has declined, according to most opinions, under the pressure of EEO laws. In fact, testing violated the candidate's right to be assessed by substantive methods. (This is not to say that all tests are trivial, but trivial uses were certainly made of them.) In other words, testing would have declined under the pressure of an increasingly litigious and sophisticated workforce even if EEO laws had never been passed. If you want an example of the prevailing opinions about testing, just consider the attitude of managers: Many top managers have never wanted to be tested at any time and have successfully resisted it.

The Decline of Application Blanks. It is commonly known that application blanks are shortened by corporate lawyers. Many questions that once seemed logical or even necessary to old-fashioned personnel officers are now "out." As discussed in Chapters 2 and 6, many of these questions are based on the logic of "social merit" and, hence, should never have been "in" the application blanks to begin with.

The Coming Decline of the Interview. It is not commonly understood that the interview is in for the same kind of rough legal weather as was testing, if not for the same reasons. A highly professional interview is certainly not trivial, but it does introduce certain inherent biases that will perhaps always effectively limit the validity of interviewers' conclusions.

This danger of making invalid judgments has been cited as a reason for training interviewers. In fact, such training programs may well succeed in preparing managers to do more effectively that which they should not be doing in the first place. Chapter 2 analyzes the serious shortcomings of the interview and proposes a better approach.

The Future of the Assessment Center. I will not attempt to predict what will happen to the assessment center. Unfortunately, it does not document a person's track record. A superb manager can in fact obtain low ratings in an assessment center. When that happens, the fat is in the fire. At that point, you have to decide what you believe to be the best evidence. In Chapter 7, I take what I trust is a very clear-cut position on the assessment center.

The Track Record: A Point of View

While the established assessment methods appear to be on shaky ground, nothing valid ever totally disappears. What is outlined in this book is not so much a way to eliminate the old methods as a program to reorganize the personnel selection process around the concept of the track record, or "TR."

A candidate's TR is, to the practical mind, the central point of assessment. We want to know what a person has done well in order to estimate the future track record. This is the way to scout professional athletes, musicians, sales personnel, and authors; it should be the way to scout managers, engineers, and other professionals.

The practical manager is very reluctant—usually refuses outright—to hire or promote someone with a poor TR. The obvious question, however, is how we determine the TR, and that is the point of this book. The practical manager needs far more than unaided intuition to know a candidate's TR of past successes and failures.

The New Sources of Knowledge
To develop effective methods for determining a candidate's track record, we can turn to the behavioral sciences and to legal precepts, drawing on some fundamental concepts that, fortunately, are coming of age just when they are needed. These research trends include:

- Life-span research—especially involving the life stages and capacities of adults.
- Behavioral technology (the study of everyday behavior and its modification through learning).
- Ecological science (the study of human behavior in relation to its external situations, and the study of how those situations are organized).

In this book, we will not attempt to examine these complex and exciting new fields in detail but will describe them briefly in the following paragraphs and draw on them when needed, especially for the insight they can give us into developing methods for knowing and evaluating a candidate's track record.

Life-span research refers to the growing body of knowledge* about the adult life-span. Whereas "human development" used to refer to knowledge of child development, the main thrust in research today is to understand how adults develop beyond their

---

* See, for example, Daniel Levinson, with Charlotte N. Darrow, Edward B. Klein, Maria H. Levinson, and Braxton McKee, *The Seasons of a Man's Life* (N.Y.: Alfred A. Knopf, 1978).

4

school years, especially including their capabilities in later life. This information is vital for framing intelligent human resources policies. An obvious example is retirement policy. The fact is—according to research—that individual differences in productivity and in health increase in later years. Two 65-year-olds have less in common in their capacity to work than two 21-year-olds. Hence, it makes little sense to retire everyone at the same age, if the retirement is based on generalized assumptions about productivity. One person can, and perhaps should, work; another might well be long overdue for retirement.

One valuable contribution of this new life-span knowledge is that it is now possible to appraise, much more factually than before, a person's status with respect to the major variables of the course of life, such as income, health, education, and learning readiness. From this factual assessment, it then becomes possible to estimate *human potential* rather than to merely use the term as a loose figure of speech. (I hasten to add that this is not the major kind of assessment we will emphasize in this book, although the appraisal of "course of life status" is indeed feasible today.)

The development of life-span research has been so rapid that it has as yet scarcely been applied in the field of personnel. It is, however, a major information resource—one that is very relevant to the possibilities outlined in this book.

Everyday observation, the second research source base for innovation in assessment, is the kind of observation made by behaviorists, among other scientists. The behaviorist typically sets up an experiment by recording simple frequencies of readily observable events. Industrial thinkers have long complained that all too many of the techniques of the behavioral sciences are remote from the workaday "real world." However, for better or for worse, the modern behaviorist spends at least part of the time observing natural settings rather than remaining in an isolated laboratory. As a result, the techniques of observation of everyday events have greatly improved over the last decade.

A good example of such a technique is the "behavioral log," in which an observer tabulates the frequency of a particular kind of event against time. If one wants to measure smoking behavior, the number of cigarettes per hour is plotted against an hour-by-hour log each day.

These methods have tremendous significance for analyzing industrial performance. They make it unnecessary, for example, to rely heavily on abstract paper-and-pencil tests or questionnaires. Instead, the modern investigator collects directly observed, concrete, and significant behavioral episodes such as "critical incidents." (Later in this chapter you will see some examples of such incidents reconstructed by executives who were attempting to review their career histories in detail.)

If the pioneer of the critical incident method was John Flanagan, the father of the log of everyday performance was B. F. Skinner. The validity of these new methods of "behavioral technology" offers great promise for potential industrial applications, including assessment for selection and promotion.

Ecological science offers a number of additional advantages. Whereas behavioral technology has important strengths, it does not provide a full appreciation of the "cognitive maps" of the job situation that the worker or manager has at all times. By knowing these maps, we can put ourselves into a person's shoes and see what steps he or she might be expected to take, while the behaviorist can only wait and see! Ecological observation is therefore quite another science. Using its methods, we can learn about the worker's daily habitat and visualize his or her actions from the worker's own viewpoint. The systematic study of workers in their work settings has been making rapid strides today, since the pioneering work of Roger Barker and Herbert Wright and, more recently, Robert Sommers.

Ecological science is applied in this book to develop systematic ways of learning about and documenting the history of a person's work settings, for it is the view here that every candidate's history consists not only of competent or incompetent "behaviors," but also of past obstacles met in the job situation.

How the New Knowledge Applies to the Track Record
The track record is the comprehensive history of the events of an employee's job performance. Every significant event—success, failure, key decision, policy change, crisis met, conflict resolved, peak experience, emotional disaster—is recaptured in a totally comprehensive history. Of course, in practical application, we take

many shortcuts and settle for far less of that comprehensive history than we might. Or according to the views of this book, we settle for knowing far less than we *should.*

Using knowledge gained through life-span research, the TR can be seen as a major subset of a person's whole life history. In the case of males, the TR is perhaps the most important part of the adult life history. True, males are not as career oriented or job centered as a few decades ago, but the TR, while somewhat less important, still appears to be dominant. In the case of a growing number of females, perhaps the same may now be said. Understanding the dynamics and phases of the career history of a manager or any other senior employee career history requires placing that career history within the larger framework of the life history. Suppose, for example, that a 50-year-old manager demands a new assignment because of an unaccountable restlessness with his job, for which he is seemingly well qualified. An understanding of the dynamics of life history might suggest that the restlessness has a cause entirely unrelated to his work or job relationships. Perhaps the manager is in a phase that will last a decade.

The track record is related to behavioral technology as well. Not only does the TR consist of major trends over a long period of time, but it also consists of countless specific events that can be described within a person's daily work life. It might seem that the number of such events, or critical incidents, is hopelessly large, and that one can never document everything that happens. Obviously, this is true. In the application of behavioral technology (such as keeping daily logs of what a manager does), we must be selective, indeed, in order not to get overwhelmed with the mass of detail.

Finally, there is the question of how the TR is illuminated by ecological science—the easiest question of all. The track record is not only a history of what the manager or other employee has done, but it is, *equally,* a history of the situations that person has faced. Hence, there is a TR of work settings. Practical managers demonstrate their knowledge of this when they insist on considering for the present job only candidates who have worked in similar environments in the past. (Of course, this rule is usually applied much too narrowly.)

To provide a very concrete illustration of how the new knowledge and methods can contribute to our understanding of employees' track records, I will briefly discuss two cases that, while fictitious, are not atypical.

The first case involves Ric, a petroleum engineer in his early fifties. He works for an oil company at a good salary but is now considering his next career move. He is most interested in obtaining a position as executive vice-president with a subsidiary. He has few self-doubts about his ability to make this happen during the next few years. He only raises the question: "Will I enjoy working within the power structure?"

In attempting to understand Ric's viewpoint and therefore to forecast the possible consequences of his next moves, you will get a little help from his résumé or the company's personnel dossier. These data only show that he has progressed rapidly in salary and status, that his performance ratings are very good, and that he has the required technical training.

To learn the real nature of Ric's strengths and limitations, we obtained two kinds of track record, or historical (on-the-job) data:

- To get a snapshot of his interpersonal relationships, we asked him for descriptions of particular situations he had faced, how he had handled them, and how they turned out. These are what John Flanagan called "critical incidents," one of which is quoted below.
- To get a "wide-angle lens" view of the way he managed projects or operations over the long run, we asked Ric for "yearly" or "project" reports prepared in specific terms. (We will not include examples of these more extended reports in this chapter because of their length but will describe them later in the book.)

Ric was asked specifically how he had handled a recent occurrence that might have broken down into a conflict. He described that critical incident as follows:

In a recent situation, I found it necessary to control my temper, although it was very difficult to do at the time. The setting for this incident is the design contractor's office in San Angelo. The project manager displayed a great deal of hostility about the oil company's becoming involved in coal operations as well as about a petroleum engineer's becoming involved in construction. The feeling of this firm had been "We're the experts—when you turn the project over to us, we'll take care of you and you shouldn't be questioning our ability or our motives."

There was a major foul-up in the design of one of the crushing facilities. The contractor's personnel hadn't spotted the problem, and the final drawings had been submitted to me for approval. I had to question their expertise, and the project manager became extremely abusive.

My first reaction was one of anger—I would have liked to hit him in the face. This was followed by my great desire to remain calm and control the situation. My options were to adjourn the meeting immediately and ask for his removal, to adjourn until he cooled down, or to continue in a calm tone of voice in a problem-solving atmosphere. I chose the latter.

The meeting ended in a better atmosphere an hour later. The results were that the management of the project improved immensely, and in future meetings with those people, everyone felt free to express disagreement without fear of being fired. (I later found out that the project manager had a problem with his health and occasionally tended to become extremely irritable.)

Before discussing what can be learned from Ric's critical incident, we should note some general characteristics about it that are strikingly different from what human resources people have traditionally recognized as data, and especially as *objective* data. Is the event Ric described "objective"? Some would say it is not, because the observer was also a participant. However, this view is not shared by many in the social and behavioral sciences. There are problems—pain, for example—that cannot be studied without participant observations.

The event is objective because it refers to something that is, at least in principle, verifiable. It occurred at a particular time and place, and several witnesses and participants who can confirm the even were present. It was a *real* event.

What can be done with this critical incident after we know about it? Among the many analyses that have been made of critical incidents, the most relevant to the purposes of this book are that we can use this event to

- Measure Ric's ability to report verifiable details.
- Characterize his interpersonal style.
- Estimate the kinds of situations he can effectively manage.

Given enough such data, the accuracy of these measurements will increase. (In this book I will mention such studies briefly, but the details of this research have been reported in my previous books and in other sources.)

To illustrate the perspective that can be gained through such data, we will now consider another, contrasting, case. This one involves Bill, an electrical engineer assigned to a physics research laboratory with the objective of building machinery to perform high-energy physics experiments.

When asked about a specific critical incident concerning his own interpersonal relationships with the laboratory staff during a time when he was attempting to get a proposal funded, Bill produced the following description:

> We were experimenting with elementary particle interaction in liquidified hydrogen near absolute zero. Each experiment involved taking up to a million photographs of these interactions. We needed to automatically and quickly "see" these events, measure them, and compute the physics data.
>
> My role was that of an electrical engineer operating on the periphery of the experiment, capable of understanding the machines if not the physics. The challenge was to match the brilliance of the physicists. The most they would say about my demonstrations was a grudging "very clever . . . very clever." I couldn't get my proposal funded. Not even at a very minimal level of a few thousand dollars. They had to save the hundreds of thousands of dollars for the physicists' projects.

By contrasting Bill's critical incident with the one described by Ric, do you get a picture of the interpersonal styles of these two engineers? Of course, you need many such incidents to be sure you are clear about what they are like, how they operate, and how well (or badly). But the data are revealing and, according to research, *predictive*. And that is the name of the game in developing selection methods.

Although it is a temptation to continue with additional illustrations of the other kinds of data that will be used in the alternative selection systems described in this book, suffice it to say that the new data are concrete, from the "real world," interesting, and produce quantitative measures of what people do and why.

Major Problems Addressed by This Book

The first, and most immediately serious, task in designing a selection system is to address the legal liabilities of the interview, which is done in the following chapter. However, avoidance of illegality is a negative reason; the positive reason for doing something about the interview's drawbacks is to develop a valid instrument for assessing job candidates.

Beyond the problem of identifying productive workers, there is the challenge of developing people. We need to understand a great deal more about individual potential, especially beyond age 35, if for no other reason than the exploding population over that age. We can now devise practical methods for studying human potential rather than just mouthing stale slogans about it. In short, the various competencies of individuals in the second half of life can be studied through the life history or, if we limit ourselves to "nine-to-five" data, through the track record.

There are, as always, additional chronic problems in selection, such as whether, through your selection policies, you are merely:

1. Cloning yourself.
2. Cloning your present workforce.
3. Choosing the "man of distinction" who looks like the whisky ads (and drinks better, perhaps, than he performs).
4. Or choosing "baby, you've come a long way," who looks like a certain cigarette ad (and smokes well but is otherwise a mistake).
5. Making careful selections at lower echelons, while permitting higher-level promotions to be made on the basis of office or company politics.

We will begin by taking a hard look at the interview and proposing a substitute system—the Track Record Inquiry—in the next several chapters. We will then examine the other selection methods—such as testing, assessment centers, application blanks, and résumés—and discuss how some of their extreme errors can be corrected through the Track Record Inquiry.

2

Replace
the Interview

In this chapter, the case against the interview will be stated and a replacement system outlined. Then in later chapters, the specifics of that system will be amplified.

The reasons for interviewing appear to be so obvious that they are rarely stated. Yet this neglect has contributed to interviewing's present vulnerability. Among the positive reasons for interviewing are the humanistic warmth it gives to an otherwise cold-blooded business procedure; its efficiency, brevity, and flexibility as a data-gathering process; and its use as a necessary negotiation tool, in case a job or promotion offer is to be made. For whatever reasons, the interview (along with the application blank) is the universal personnel selection method.

But when attempts are made to validate the interview, its flaws begin to appear. The disturbing findings of E. C. Webster are typical. Canadian army officers interviewed candidates for officers' training school, with the officers' decisions being recorded throughout the hour spent with each candidate. Analysis of these records later revealed that the officers typically made a firm decision only four minutes after the start of the interview. Their initial impressions were apparently not disturbed during the remaining 56 minutes (which were presumably devoted to maintaining good public relations), but what can be assumed about the validity of such quick decisions?

Validity studies—over the last generation—have repeatedly failed to confirm the wisdom of placing great reliance on the interview. I have reviewed six major papers (written every few years by different scholars who digested the validation evidence), and not one confirms the soundness of interviewing as ordinarily practiced.*

Among the options, with respect to the interview, are:

- To leave the interview alone, since no one knows how to do without it or what to do to improve it.
- To train people to do a better job of interviewing. (There is no evidence that this improves the interview's validity. There *is* evidence that trainees apply what they have learned, but not that the design learned produces valid predictions.)
- To give the interview more "structure."
- To de-emphasize the interview.

The proposal presented in this chapter—and amplified throughout the book—combines the last three options. First, we must find a structure that is legally and scientifically defensible. It should be one that does not emphasize the interpersonal factors that now cause so much variability in interview results. In that sense, de-emphasize the interview. Finally, we must devise a way to train decision makers to use the newly designed procedure.

We cannot leave the interview as it is if we want valid selection decisions. To do so is to risk legal challenges, since the courts—and many aggressive attorneys—read the research evidence that I have cited above.

What Is Wrong with Interviewing?

The major shortcomings of interviewing can be found in its emphasis on prestige (or social merit), its reliance on the interviewer's ability to judge and interpret the candidate's personality and non-verbal cues, its reliance on imprecise trait ratings, and—in short—the inflated expectations that are associated with the entire interviewing process. We will now consider each of these factors.

* See Richard D. Arvey, "Unfair Discrimination in the Employment Interview: Legal and Psychological Aspects," *Psychological Bulletin*, July 1979, pp. 736–765; and Charles A. Dailey, *Panel Assessment for Promotion* (Boston: Biodata, Inc., 1977).

Emphasis on Social Merit

The first—and major—fault of the interview is the intrusion of subjective notions of human quality on the interviewer's judgment. Any society defines certain marks of "quality," and persons who show those marks are given preference in a variety of ways. For example, certain tribes accord greater prestige (or social merit) to a warrior with more scarification on his body. In most societies, age and (male) sex receive status preference.

This idea of social merit is exemplified in the term "qualified." The personnel officer says a certain candidate should be hired because he or she is "better qualified." What does this mean? It is usual to say that the candidate is better qualified because he or she is better qualified: circular reasoning meaning that the personnel officer simply chooses to prefer that person. We will, in that case, usually find that the decision reflects one or more of the criteria listed in Figure 1.

In other cases, the personnel officer may well be able to define what is meant by "qualification," but the explanation may not be valid. For example, naval officers used to have to be "able-bodied." A one-armed candidate would therefore be "washed out," in spite of the fact that he or she might well possess talents in short supply. The tradition of hiring naval officers who had all their limbs (or two eyes, etc.) reflected ancient prejudices about what "gentlemen" and officers should look like and what physical strength they should possess.

Granted that any society has a status or preference system. Why is this thinking extended to control who receives jobs or promotions, however, when the status system has nothing to do with the factors responsible for excellence in performance?

Figure 1 shows two kinds of "qualifications." One kind is used to include people, the other kind, to exclude them. The logic is the same: We want to hire "better-qualified" people, but we don't want to say exactly what that means. To test the items listed to see which ones you consider valid, just ask yourself these questions:

- If this statement were true of a candidate, would the candidate have a better chance to be selected for any given job? My job, for example?

14

Figure 1. "Social merit" criteria.

Review the factors below, placing a check mark beside those criteria you think most firms use to *favor* some applicants over others and placing an X beside those criteria you think are often used to *reject* applicants.

____ 1. A person's language and dialect sound like those of people from a small town.

____ 2. A male applicant has an athletic appearance.

____ 3. A person has a degree from a highly respected college.

____ 4. A male applicant is 5'1".

____ 5. An applicant is very well dressed.

____ 6. A person has a criminal record but presents evidence of having "gone straight" for the past five years.

____ 7. An applicant is 50 years old.

____ 8. An applicant is 25 percent overweight but otherwise healthy.

____ 9. A person's father is a high-status professional, well known in the city or town.

____ 10. A male applicant is married.

____ 11. A person's grades in high school were somewhat below average.

____ 12. A person has a bad (slightly unpleasant) complexion.

____ 13. A female applicant is 6'2".

____ 14. A female applicant is extremely good looking.

____ 15. An applicant has changed jobs three times in the last two years.

____ 16. A person needs a job (that is, the person is now unemployed).

____ 17. A female applicant has two young children.

____ 18. A male applicant has two young children.

____ 19. An applicant does not easily look you in the eye.

____ 20. An applicant has a mild stutter.

____ 21. An applicant has often been overdrawn at the bank.

____ 22. An applicant is known to have brought an Equal Employment Opportunity (EEO) suit alleging age discrimination.

____ 23. An applicant is known to have brought an EEO suit alleging reverse discrimination.

____ 24. An applicant worked actively for or against nuclear power.

____ 25. An applicant presents good letters of recommendation from the local bank president in his small town, his minister, and his previous employer.

- If the statement were true, would the candidate have a worse chance to be selected?

I have shown Figure 1 to many managers concerned with employment and promotion. The average manager checks or X-es more than half the items, often saying "I have jobs that *require* this characteristic. People like this perform better." Consider this fact: Taller men are hired more often. But are there not jobs in which male height does not represent a performance advantage? In sales, it is typically thought that people buy more from manly men and cuddly soft women. But are there not products better sold by nonthreatening males and by dominant-looking females? From a business standpoint, hadn't you better base selection decisions about the people involved with *your* product line and services on *accurate* information rather than on stereotyped generalizations?

At this point, some personnel readers may assume that I am leading up to the fact that some of the criteria shown in Figure 1 are illegal, and they know that. They have been following the court rulings. But the issue of discrimination is only the small tip of a large iceberg. The hidden iceberg is social merit.

The use of social merit criteria is largely legal—but largely invalid. We will also consider some instances in which social merit criteria are apparently valid on the surface but, when examined more closely, are found to be destructive of the objective of interviewing. Three kinds of social merit criteria are presented in Figure 1:

1. Elitist: the policy of hiring or promoting persons with advantages, thereby maintaining a system of past privilege.
2. Egocentric: the policy of hiring or promoting persons like the interviewer (usually under the guise of selecting those who will "fit in").
3. General: the policy of hiring or promoting persons typically considered "better" in society.

The net result of such policies is to confer advantages on those who already have them. This result resembles the situation in banking where credit or loans are most easily obtained by those who need the least. This policy is certainly in the interest of the banks and, on the surface, is valid. However, the policies listed above are essentially divisive and convey hidden messages to workers that, I maintain, will reduce productivity—as the workers see the selection system rewarding candidates for their characteristics and not for their track records.

Are these biased selection policies actually followed? Do they really influence interviewer judgments? The unconscious influence of social merit criteria is actually a factor, as shown in a classic little experiment I like to cite. The experimenter set out to measure the influence of social prestige on the suggestibility of crowds. Dressed as a bum, the experimenter stood awkwardly on a street corner among a small crowd waiting for the "Don't Walk" sign to change to "Walk." Apparently becoming impatient, he started impulsively across the street without waiting for "Walk." A confederate nearby noted the number of people in the crowd who immediately followed the experimenter in this action (few or none did). Next the experimenter changed to an elitist garb. The same man, now well dressed, awaited the same "Walk" sign in a new crowd. You can now guess the rest of the experiment: The confederate's notes showed that many more people in the crowd followed the well-dressed experimenter when he again stepped impulsively off the curb.

But isn't there some validity to awarding snob points (to the graduates of elite schools), peer points (to people like the interviewer with a similar upbringing), or general points (to "qualified" candidates)? The phrases "better people," "good ol' boys," and "qualified candidates" are circular: Their validity is unproved. But even if they proved valid, they pass on signals to others—signals that the track record does not matter; that the rich or advantaged get richer or more advantaged; that you hire or promote your buddies; that *connections* count.

I suggested earlier that social merit considerations unconsciously intrude upon the interviewer's judgments. I believe that such considerations do intrude. But how *unconscious* is the intrusion? Most seasoned managers who have looked at Figure 1 endorsed it as describing how the personnel selection process actually works and what values it embodies.

The first thing wrong with the interview, then, is that it is typically regarded as an opportunity to directly observe a candidate—through listening and interaction—in order to size up the candidate's social merits, decide whether he or she is "our sort," and determine whether the interviewer will look bad by hiring a person not admired or desired by others. Once again, what is wrong with hiring or promoting "beautiful people"? Very simply:

1. There is nothing wrong with being "beautiful people," or with preferring them.
2. What *is* wrong is to confuse a person's *social status* with his or her performance.

Reliance on Judging Personality
A second flaw in the interview is its psychiatric legacy. Perhaps nothing is more difficult than the psychiatrist's or psychoanalyst's probing for hidden meanings and attempting to evaluate personalities. Don't we need to know "personality" in order to fill positions, to avoid persons with abnormal problems, and in general, to understand job candidates?

These might seem to be worthy goals, but I have two objections to them. First, such knowledge would not appear to be necessary for estimating a person's future performance. Second, there are serious doubts—raised by students of psychiatry itself—that the psychiatric method of interviewing is valid for understanding personality. We see this method at its worst in the courtroom, when the prosecutor in, say, a murder case brings in psychiatric experts to testify that the accused was sane when he or she killed the victim. The defense then brings in its *own* experts to testify to the opposite.

The influence that psychiatry had upon the design of interviewing is perhaps one of the interview's most serious weaknesses.

Reliance on Nonverbal Cues
A third and related fault of interviewing is the interviewer's tendency to look for nonverbal cues. Many interviewer training programs solemnly teach this skill. It is an interesting parlor game and a pastime endlessly practiced in singles bars. I do not doubt that research into the "silent language"—the cues which are transmit-

ted by gestures—is interesting. I do doubt, however, that these clues have been proved valid enough to serve as the basis for allocating jobs or promotions.

We all have our favorite cues or clues. One manager took prospective sales candidates to lunch before making any final decisions. Seating himself directly across the table from the candidate, the manager particularly observed the person's use of the knife to slice steak or fish. The "key" cue was whether the candidate sliced in a direction across his or her body (an indication that the candidate was "inhibiting aggression" and would therefore lack the assertiveness necessary for selling) or slicing in a direction toward the manager (an indication that the candidate was "releasing aggression" and would therefore be a good prospect for a sales position). (As for vegetarians, the manager would not hire them. Having nothing to slice, they failed the crucial knife-test.)

Will research into silent language ever develop enough to warrant your reading nonverbal signals to understand the "inner person"? I doubt it, if only because the one thing shown true of the silent language is that it varies with the culture. You would have to learn a new set of cues for every cultural or ethnic group you encounter. In the meantime, *I* would not want to have to defend your decisions in court.

Somewhat more mischievous is the nonverbal testing instrument, such as the polygraph. It is being sold to businesses that want to avoid hiring candidates who will pilfer or lie. However, the polygraph is not actually and literally a lie detector, as the seasoned operator must admit. Rather, it monitors the fluctuations in different bodily systems. Blood pressure, for example, goes up or down for many reasons, and yours may or may not go up when you lie. (If it does, you can still learn how to consciously control blood pressure as well as many other body functions formerly thought to be unconscious and automatic.)

My main point is not whether the polygraph actually detects lies, but, if this precise instrument cannot specifically detect inner states (which it cannot), why you believe *you* can. What can you as an interviewer conclude from observing the candidate as he or she flushes, stammers, coughs nervously, shakes hands wetly or dryly, sits close or far away, and does or does not interrupt you? If such cues cannot reveal the candidate's inner state of mind, how little can they reveal about future job performance?

Reliance on Imprecise Trait Ratings

The result of selection interviewing is usually a set of ratings of impressions, or trait ratings. We want "leaders," so the interviewer rates "leadership." We want "initiative," so the interviewer rates that. The interviewer realizes these traits are a bit broad and vague, but he or she knows the line managers have asked for reports based on them as if they were real, and the interviewer believes that a mere impression gains precision by being quantified. Hence, the interviewer—who might feel embarrassed if asked to prove that a candidate has "leadership" qualities—feels comfortable reporting that the candidate's leadership rating is "3."

Trait ratings, according to Walter Mischel, only reflect the perceiver's theory. For example, suppose I do see evidence that a candidate is articulate with words. I rate him a "1" in articulateness with words. I do not see evidence that he is otherwise intelligent—nor do I see proof that he is not. What I will then do is to rate intelligence also a "1" (instead of declining to rate that which I do not observe). This rating is given not on the basis of evidence but on the basis of my theory that being articulate with words is part of, or correlated with, intelligence. This is called "going beyond the evidence."

It is good fun to express your theories, but it is unfair to give or deny work because of them. Of course, not only interviewers rate traits. Other kinds of selection systems—such as assessment centers—also rate traits, and we will examine their problems in a later chapter.

Inflated Expectations

Related to the above faults are the lofty hopes and expectations of selection interviewers. Instead of seeking to collect tangible evidence from a candidate, the interviewer seeks to know a person, to evaluate his or her inner qualities, or even to estimate the person's long-range potential.

It's too much. Interviewing fails because it is too hard to do. Its failures are self-imposed and result from the inflated expectations for interviewing—expectations that are uncorrected by reality (because they are too vague to be corrected), that are at times mysterious, and that in any event permit all too much leeway for biased social values to distort the collection of objective evidence.

The Track Record Inquiry: A Simpler System

One way to lower the expectations of managers and personnel professionals is to define the selection task as one of documenting the candidate's track record. This definition lowers such expectations as "getting to know" the candidate or estimating his or her character, but at the same time it increases the expectations of producing valid and reliable decisions.

The principal differences between the traditional interview system and the proposed "Track Record Inquiry" (or "TRI") approach can be summarized as follows:

Traditional Interview	*Track Record Inquiry*
1. Design is influenced by psychiatry and the social sciences.	1. Design is influenced by law and managerial theory.
2. Judging the candidate's personality characteristics, such as motivation, interest, and ability, is emphasized.	2. Obtaining evidence of the candidate's work performance, such as results and how they were accomplished, is emphasized.
3. A heavy burden is placed on the interviewer to obtain valid impressions.	3. The burden for providing evidence is transferred to the candidate, but the interviewer remains responsible for seeing that the evidence is judged validly.
4. Validation and reliability studies show that this interview method fails.	4. Validation of historical (track record) data is promising, as will be discussed in later chapters.

Traditional Interview	*Track Record Inquiry*
5. The interviewer does not feel responsible for producing evidence to support his or her conclusions.	5. The interviewer must be able to prove where the conclusions came from.
6. End result: a set of ratings or an impression.	6. End result: evidence of a candidate's past performance in relevant situations.

Main Features of the Track Record Inquiry
The main features of the TRI can be found in what the inquiry attempts to accomplish, where the approach originated, in the shifting of the burden of the selection process from the employer to the candidate, and in the separation of data collection from evaluation. These features will be examined briefly in the following paragraphs.

Aims of the Track Record Inquiry. In conducting a Track Record Inquiry, you will have done a good job if the candidate has fully reconstructed his or her work history and presented the best defensible case for his or her candidacy. You do not have to make judgments (that comes later). Free of the burden of judging at this point, you can devote your full attention to counseling the candidate on how to present you with the best case—based on credible, solid, detailed information relevant to the job.

Origins of the Track Record Inquiry. The TRI approach grew out of recent legal pressures on business firms to defend their selection judgments and out of management theory. EEO and employment rights laws are still growing, but clearly an employer's day of making arbitrary decisions about hiring and promotion is ending, if not yet ended. In contrast, the interview grew out of the standards of social merit and psychiatric judgment with their many weaknesses.

The legal origin of TRI shows most clearly in the central concept or evidence (the track record is evidence) that the law demands. The origin of TRI in management theory shows most clearly in the concept of the job model (see the next chapter), which is structured according to the management by objectives approach.

And finally, the behavioral sciences have also made valuable contributions to the development of the TRI approach, especially through the insights provided by newer work in social psychology, such as in attribution.

Burden of the Track Record Inquiry. The Track Record Inquiry is easier to conduct than the interview, because the burden has largely been passed to the candidate. We say, in effect, "You are the one seeking this position. *You* tell *me* why you can do the job." I do not mean to be negative in saying this. Because—as I shall explain in subsequent chapters—the rest of the role of the person conducting the inquiry is that of counselor, supporting the candidate's efforts to find and present the most convincing and relevant case. But the counselor need not *extract* information from the candidate nor *guess* what is in the candidate's head or past history.

If the TRI is easier to do, then we should reasonably expect greater reliability from it. That is, the track record is history; it should contain verifiable facts. Such verification, done as research (it can't be routinely done within the employment process), has shown that track record information is indeed reliable. For example, we questioned the previous three bosses of each of 55 candidates for promotion in a Commonwealth of Massachusetts project. These bosses were asked to volunteer descriptions of the factual results of the candidates' work during each of three one-year periods. These descriptions confirmed 90 percent of what the candidates said.

Separation of Data Collection from Judgment. The track record is reconstructed by the candidate after you show how and why this is done. You can then record it as the candidate describes it to you or have the candidate write it out. As counselor, you make no ratings at all at this point. The objectivity of the track record is not clouded by the impressionism of your evaluation. Just as a trial in a court of law consists of carefully regulated presentation of evidence by attorneys and witnesses, under the supervision of a judge and following rules, so data collection in the selection process can be made to proceed.

Judgment of this track record presented by the candidate is

made later, after the evidence is in. Just as in a court of law, where the jury rates the evidence (not the judge, attorneys, and witnesses), someone other than the counselor can judge the TR. There are separate skills used in judging, and separate training is required for it. Of course, there are situations in which a single person must both collect and judge the data. The important thing is to remember that two *different* functions are involved.

Advantages of the Track Record Inquiry

Because of the differences between data collection done during interviews and data collection done as part of the Track Record Inquiry, the TRI offers the following advantages:

1. It is legally more defensible because of its objectivity and its explicit rules for collecting evidence (which will be described in the following chapters).
2. It is easier because the burden of data presentation is on the candidate (who else *can* know the track record?).
3. It is more understandable to managers because of the influence of management concepts on the design of the TRI (also discussed in the next chapter) and because most managers naturally sympathize with the track record concept.
4. It is easier to learn and to conduct than the interview because data collection is separated from the judgment process.
5. It is more job relevant because (as the next two chapters will show) the track record is structured in terms of the job sought.

These points represent advantages that the Track Record Inquiry has over interviewing and do not necessarily pertain to the issues raised in later chapters on the TRI versus other methods, such as assessment centers.

The Minor but Indispensable Role of Traditional Interviewing

In spite of the above arguments against interviewing, I do not propose that it be totally replaced. Rather, its influence on the final selection decisions should be reduced. There are, in fact, indispensable contributions to be made by the one-on-one conversation in hiring and promotion.

USING THE TRACK RECORD APPROACH

The Key to Successful Personnel Selection

At last there's help for managers and personnel specialists who spend a good deal of time in nonproductive interviews! USING THE TRACK RECORD APPROACH describes a proven, practical method for selecting the most qualified candidates—new hires as well as transfers and promotions from within—quickly and in complete compliance with EEO/Affirmative Action requirements.

With this step-by-step system, you'll see how to get applicants to present to you their proven TRACK RECORD...performance data and critical incidents that relate directly to the job in question. You'll not only spot the right people faster, but you can bet they are the ones who will be the most capable and productive on the job.

Find out how the TRACK RECORD APPROACH—

- *Forces* the applicant to make the best case for his or her candidacy
- *Gives* you better data for decision making and ample evidence to support your decisions should they be challenged
- *Documents* the information on which hiring decisions—and promotion decisions—are made
- *Reduces* the cost of hiring and training employees
- *Eliminates* needless red tape, legal hassles, and interviews that lead nowhere
- Makes it plain to all concerned that you are not influenced by bias, social status, or appearance
- Saves screening and interviewing time

USING THE TRACK RECORD APPROACH also provides questionnaires, models, charts, forms, graphs, and case histories to help you grasp the system and use it effectively.

amacom... *for excellence in management*

AMERICAN MANAGEMENT ASSOCIATIONS
135 West 50th Street, New York, N.Y. 10020

For example, our ethical sense would be outraged if a decision were made denying us a job or promotion without a hearing. This outrage would be similar to the feelings we would have about condemnation without a trial. We have the right to confront our "accuser."

Someone would have to meet with a candidate one-on-one to explain any selection method—including TRI.

The counseling problems that arise in employment can only be handled one-on-one.

Consider a position requiring effective interpersonal skills. Here the interview provides an indispensable opportunity to observe the candidate as he or she demonstrates those skills. In that case, be sure the interview does in fact sample the relevant human interaction skills. For example, if you are hiring a foreman or forewoman who will need skills to deal with production workers, do *you*—the interviewer—really so closely resemble those workers that the candidate's skill in dealing with you can be considered a fair sample of his or her skill in dealing with the workers?

Finally, traditional interviewing or one-on-one conversation is indispensable in making or negotiating a job offer.

3

First, You Need
a Job Model

You cannot hit a target without clearly perceiving its outline. In the
personnel selection process, the "target" (the job) must be defined
by the people who want the job done. What is the candidate
supposed to do, or—even more basic—why does the job exist in
the first place? The superiors, however, may be too far removed
from the way a job is best done to outline it precisely. A still greater
problem is line managers' lack of patience with this precision work;
they would rather leave it to "personnel."

Over the decades since professional personnel administrators
first began to take on the assignment of preparing the job description, the instrument has evolved into an important document,
meeting many vital purposes: among them, job classification, job
evaluation, and organization analysis. However, these purposes
do not appear to include the precise definition of a selection target.
To develop a better instrument (which will be called the "job
model" here), we should take a good look at what the job description does not and cannot say—but what we must know in order to
make an accurate candidate selection for that job.

Some authorities use "job specifications" to define the kind of
person who can do the work in a job description. For a particular
position, we might specify an engineer with experience in Venezu-
elan oil exploration, for example. However, the job specification is
no better than the job description allows it to be. Moreover, many
job specifications—perhaps all of them—are lists of "social merits"
in the sense in which the term was used in the preceding chapter.
This means that they orient the selection process toward nonbusi-

ness purposes, which is to say they essentially maintain social privilege rather than identify people who can perform.

Limitations of the Job Description

Line managers often ignore job descriptions. They go ahead and assign whatever work they please, whether it is in the "JD" or not. For the employee's part, he or she knows that much of the day is spent doing things not in the description. If the job is what the manager decides should be done—or what the employee actually does—then what does the job description *describe*?

The job description's unreality does not end there. Because the conventional unit of the JD is a "duty," the JD loses its link to the original *purposes* of the job. That is, the purpose of a job is never to perform duties. This is a circular notion that would make an activity its own purpose—a good definition for a hobby but a poor one for a job!

How could an unreal document provide a precise selection target?

Several attempts have been made in personnel administration to correct these faults in the job description. Perhaps the most sophisticated recent attempt has been to amplify duties—to make them more precise.

Behavioral Standards

What will make a job description into an adequate selection tool? It is common to say that if duties are specified, in terms of "behavioral standards," they become much more useful. This may be true, but this improvement still does not make them useful for selecting personnel.

A behavioral standard simply specifies the way a duty is performed if it is well done. For example, if making coffee were a duty, the behavioral standards might include:

- Having at least half a pot available at all times.
- Having the first pot ready by the time the first guest arrives in the morning.
- Having enough cups for everyone who wants coffee.

But notice that the duty of making coffee may not be a legitimate purpose of this particular job in the first place. In that case, the behavioral standard only quantifies or specifies what is not a valid requirement.

Results and Job Environment: The Missing Factors

What is missing in the traditional job description (and also in job specifications) are the results sought in setting up the job in the first place. These are the tangible products of the job or the legitimate business reasons for having the job. In a public service job, results refer to the services that were legislated in authorizing the job.

For reasons too lengthy to summarize here, I recommend that you limit results to economic outcomes (such as making sales), production (of a product or a service), innovation, or preservation of the organization's assets (including its cohesion and its money). These results should be as tangible as possible, and they should not be described in terms of the activity by which they are produced. For example, the results provided by a typist are not *typing*, but letters. Writing letters from one typist to another would not be a (valid) result. However, letters concerning the improvement of production would be a result. Producing letters concerning the Christmas party would not be. And so on.

Results are not enough if our job model is to describe the reality of the work. It is also necessary to define what makes the job hard or easy. (If this is *not* a significant consideration, then there is no selection problem—anyone could do the job.)

Ordinarily, if you ask a person what makes his or her job hard, you will hear about obstructions, such as a difficult boss, lack of tools or information, or interruptions—all outside interferences.

All these outside factors can be combined under the heading "job environment." The job environment includes all the factors not under the employee's direct control that influence performance. We cannot select a candidate without knowing the job environment. We must select for the situations that will actually be faced by the person trying to do the work.

The Job Model: What It Is, What It Looks Like

We are now ready to say what is meant by a "job model" and how it is used in personnel selection: The job model specifies the results sought and the job environment. These are its major differences from the job description. Of course the job model also mentions the duties or actions to be performed—but only as they relate to overcoming environmental obstacles and attaining the stated results.

This may not sound like a major difference from the traditional job description, but it is in fact a complete reorganization of the concept. Since we are no longer talking about "duties," we need a new word. We can use the term "action" to refer to an environmentally suited and result-seeking activity. The job model, in short, prescribes *actions*.

If your idea of selection is to identify a person who will obtain results, you need a job model designed to guide that selection. That is:

- To predict results, you must know the obstacles to attaining those results, and you must know whether the candidate can and will carry out the actions required to overcome those obstacles.
- You ought to select those candidates for whom you predict results.

To serve as a valid framework for prediction of performance, job models must be "honest." That is, if there is a significant environmental factor that may hinder performance, it may not be omitted. If it is, the prediction will fail. Seasoned personnel officers can easily give examples of such factors that are talked about but not written down. One is a stupid, unreasonable, or incompetent boss. You will never find that in a job description. And yet it is necessary to consider this major "environmental" obstacle to good performance.

A job model does not have to meet any of the purposes of the job description: It does not need to classify the job, evaluate it, analyze it, or clean it up by omitting tabooed facts about obstacles to performance. It merely needs to tell as much of the essential truth about how a person becomes successful in that job as can be briefly recorded, in order that a potentially effective candidate can be recognized.

But how is this recognition to take place? It is not simple. Such a match-up will be given rather detailed attention in a later chapter. Here we will let it suffice to say that a candidate who has effectively produced results in a particular environment before is assumed to be able to do it again. If this simple principle is accepted, then we recognize a good candidate not by whether he or she meets certain "job specifications" but by whether in the past that candidate has

- Often, recently, persistently, and convincingly
- Attained the specified results
- In environments as hard as this one.

Note that this definition says nothing about the candidate's skills or knowledge. It is assumed that if this definition is true, the candidate must have those skills or knowledge. However, the belief among personnel selection experts that one must have "skills, ability, knowledge, and competence" is so strong that I am willing to add the qualification that

- If we do not know whether the candidate has obtained equivalent results in an equivalent environment, we must then obtain other evidence that the candidate has skills, knowledge, ability, and competence like those named in the job model.

A job model therefore states the requirements in a brief form so that we can match them against the track record of the candidate before us.

Sample job models are shown in Figures 2 and 3. (The reason for their format will become clear in a later chapter, when we examine a form that is convenient for recording information during the Track Record Inquiry.) Each job model consists of a list of the results to be obtained, statements of the environment (the external supports available for the person in the job—and the obstacles confronting him or her), and the actions (skilled, competent, able, knowledgeable, effortful, etc.) required by that environment.

Figure 2. Sample job model: route sales representative.

RESULTS SOUGHT:	A. Maintain delivery schedules B. Deal with customer complaints and retain old customers. C. Obtain new customers. D. Increase the shelf space given to our products in the largest supermarkets. E. Make sure merchandise is fresh.
JOB ENVIRONMENT:	The routes available are in a combined industrial and residential area. This makes driving schedules hard to maintain, especially when shifts let out. It also imposes a number of low-volume stops on the routes, which makes it even more necessary to concentrate on the more promising locations. There is a problem of fatigue on this job, such that the position has a high turnover rate.
PRIORITY ACTIONS:	The successful route sales representative will need to be better at planning time and managing fatigue than most are. Knowledge of the grocery store business problems that are characteristic of such areas is essential. The representative will need to work with the route record book as follows . . .

Building a Job Model

In many ways, building a job model is similar to the interviewing process conducted by Studs Terkel in *Working*.* He talked to people in diverse occupations about what they did all day, and how they felt about it. A job model, unlike a job description, is a very human document; it should tell the truth about a job. I had the strong impression Terkel's informants *were* telling him the truth.

However, it is understandable that many of the readers of this book are systematically and functionally oriented. They want to read about steps to be taken and the reasons why they must be taken in a particular order and not in some other order. And those

---

* New York: Pantheon Books, 1974.

Figure 3. Sample job model: police chief.

RESULTS SOUGHT:	A. Increase the speed with which major offenders are arrested, especially those who have been violent toward children, older persons, and women, or who peddle drugs.
	B. Lower the rates of violent incidents between persons who are strangers.
	C. Lower the rates of violent incidents between family members.
	D. Provide speedy and fair response to citizen complaints about the police.
	E. Deploy adequate forces to priority areas, accurately estimating the probable pressures on the police.
JOB ENVIRONMENT:	The job is located in an urban area bordering a beach resort area that includes a gambling casino. Citizen support for the police has in recent years declined as union organizing has become more visible, especially since the numerous job actions during the last year. The current mayor is attempting to get court rulings that will breach the confidentiality of police investigations . . .
PRIORITY ACTIONS:	In light of the above, we need a chief who is able to restore public confidence and understanding of the problems of managing a police force in such an area. During the next few months, the chief will need to devote most of his or her time to . . .

---

are legitimate orientations provided it is remembered that the human—emotional, motivational, attitudinal, informal—side of work is neglected only at the price of a major loss in validity. If job descriptions tell us bureaucratic lies, they cannot help us predict performance.

The form shown in Figure 4 outlines the five steps required to produce a job model. These steps are designed to help you systematically arrive at the point where you can describe precisely what a job requires. Before discussing the process, however, we need to consider where to obtain the information to complete the form.

Figure 4. Job-model building.

Step One: Results (or Goals)

1. Complete the following sentence in eight ways:

    A person in this job is effective if he or she produces
    the result* that . . .

		(a)	(b)
A.	_____		
	_____	___	___
B.	_____		
	_____	___	___
C.	_____		
	_____	___	___
D.	_____		
	_____	___	___
E.	_____		
	_____	___	___
F.	_____		
	_____	___	___
G.	_____		
	_____	___	___
H.	_____		
	_____	___	___

2. Now rank order the eight goals by importance by putting numbers in column (a). The most important goal is 1, the next most important is 2, and so on down to 8, the least important.

3. Finally, rank order the eight goals by difficulty by putting numbers in column (b). The most difficult result to attain is 1, the next most difficult is 2, and so on down to 8, the easiest.

    * A "result" should be a very *tangible* effect of work, *useful to someone else* and contributing to the organization's reasons for existing. (For example, a sale is a more valid result than is a sales manual, because an organization is more likely to be in business to get something sold than to write a manual about selling.)

Step Two: Work Environment

1. Characterize the work setting for this job by listing in detail* the "field forces" that facilitate or hinder performance. These are the positive and negative environmental factors—such as policies, people, budget, equipment, and data.

+ Field Forces	− Field Forces

2. Please go back and number the forces in importance from 1 + (the most important positive field force) to 3 +, and from 1 − (the most important negative field force) to 3 −.

Step Three: Job Demands

Complete the following sentences with the most appropriate statement that occurs to you. It should, if possible, be the single feature, or demand, that is most *crucial* to doing the job well. Or it could be a feature that might be likely to cause many people to fail. Leave a space blank if nothing occurs to you.

1. The person in this position must work effectively with

   A. a boss who _____

   _____

* By "detail" we mean more than general terms like "people" or "policies." Be specific enough so that it is readily apparent *what* policies, *which* people, etc.

B. subordinates who _____

_____

C. associates who _____

_____

D. people outside the organization who _____

_____

E. committees or boards that _____

_____

F. a department, plant, or division of the organization that _____

_____

G. an organization that _____

_____

H. outside (client, community, government) organizations that _____

_____

2. The person in this position must be effective in working with

   I. new concepts of _____

_____

   J. words, in making oral presentations about _____

_____

   K. words, in presenting written presentations about _____

_____

   L. financial or cost data regarding _____

_____

   M. numerical or mathematical data regarding _____

_____

3. The person in this position must be effective in

   N. coping with physical demands or stresses associated with _____

_____

O. working creatively with things or crafts, such as _____

_____

P. working with equipment, such as _____

_____

Step Four: Job Demands (Prioritized)

Review the 16 statements you made in Step Three. Make the following decisions and record them in the appropriate column.

1. Choose *8* of the 16 statements about job demands that are more important to effectiveness and write the letter corresponding to each statement on the following lines:

   More Important Demands: ___ ___ ___ ___ ___ ___ ___ ___

2. Choose *4* of those 8 statements as being still more important, and write their letters below.

   Most Important Demands: ___ ___ ___ ___

3. Choose *2* of these 4 statements as being of the greatest importance, and write their letters below.

   Two Most Critically Important Demands: ___ ___

4. Choose *one* of these 2 statements as being the single most important statement in the list, and write its letter below.

   Most Critically Important Demand: ___

Step Five: Motivations

In light of the job demands listed in Step Four, consider the kinds and intensity of the motivations required for this job. Rate each statement below by selecting the rating number from the following five-point scale that best characterizes the degree to which this particular job requires the motivation described, and mark each rating number in the column to the right of the statements.

1. This job makes very intense demands for this motivation.
2. This job makes high demands for this motivation.
3. This job makes average demands for this motivation.
4. This job makes low demands for this motivation.
5. This job does not require this motivation.

A. The person in this job must want to produce a stable level of performance and be satisfied to work within routines and seek reliability.

B. The person in this job must need people—need their goodwill and affection—and care a great deal about having close relationships. ___

C. The person in this job must want to acquire and use influence, maintain control over the organization and the operation, and exercise leadership. ___

D. The person in this job must want to do something better and concentrate on setting objectives so that progress can be measured fairly quickly and directly. ___

E. The person in this job must want to deepen his or her experiences, intensify them, and broaden his or her consciousness of what is happening in the job environment. ___

Building a job model essentially requires information about the purposes for which the job was originally designed (that is, the results, or goals, that must be accomplished) and about the actual pressures and dynamics of the work itself (the obstacles to performance, the relationships, the required actions, and the motivations). The boss is the primary source of data on job goals and results: He or she knows why the job exists. The data about the actual job pressures and forces, however, can best be obtained from the worker—the person who has directly experienced them. (With respect to motivation, probably the *best* workers have the greatest understanding of the kinds of motivation that produce solid results.)

In short, the worker—who will be most knowledgeable about the job pressures and forces—cannot always know the fundamental purposes of the job, and the boss—who will be the most knowledgeable about the job's purpose—may not fully appreciate the day-to-day realities of the work. Hence, the boss and the worker *together* can usually build a job model far more effectively than can either alone. (Certainly the personnel department alone can provide very little of the required information.)

We will now examine each of the steps shown in Figure 4 for building a job model.

Step One: Results (or Goals)

Step One is designed to help you describe the goals, or end results, expected in the job. The format of the step is oriented toward the boss who cannot always say clearly why a job exists. In my experience, such a boss can be quite embarrassed by having his or her ignorance exposed. Since the boss may not even have set up the job originally, asking for its desired results may not seem like a fair question. For these reasons, a casual, "thought starter" sentence completion procedure is used. It is a bit less abrupt and annoying than straightway asking for a prioritized listing of the job's goals.

The order in which the goals, or results, are initially recorded is not important. (Goal A is not more important than goal B; it is just the first one that occurred to the person filling out the form.) The relative importance is ranked after the goals have been written down.

(There is no need to limit yourself to exactly eight goals, but it is important to try to think of at least that many, to be sure that some vital purpose is not left out that will have to be added later.) Once the goals have been listed and ranked by importance, they are ranked by difficulty, to prepare the person providing the information for the following step.

Step Two: Work Environment
Step Two is designed to help you describe the work environment, or the setting for the job. This description is developed in terms of the positive and negative "field forces"—those factors in the work situation that facilitate or hinder effective job performance.

Who is the best person to describe the environment? There is probably no general answer, but most likely it would be a seasoned person, or someone who has done the job in the past. It is not necessary that the person providing the information about the work setting have been successful in the job. Sometimes the person most aware of obstacles is the one who is failing.

There would, however, be one exception to the generalization that a seasoned person should describe the field forces. That is the case in which there has been a large turnover during the early months on the job, when a new person encounters so many discouraging obstacles. In that case, the best person to describe the work environment would be a fairly new worker; seasoned workers often forget how hard it is to get started.

Step Three: Job Demands

Step Three, which is designed to help you identify the job demands, presents a series of incomplete sentences. The respondent is asked to complete each one by describing a demand, or feature, associated with the job that is crucial to effectiveness.

The incomplete sentences are divided into three broad groups according to whether each demand referred to involves

- Working with people (sentences A through H).
- Working with concepts—mainly words and numbers (sentences I through M).
- Working with physical demands and things (sentences N through P).

This division, which is based on one of the major approaches to job analysis, stimulates the respondent to consider the various ways in which effective action takes place. This format is not a personality test, but merely an efficient way of quickly describing the complex requirements of many types of jobs.

Step Four: Job Demands (Prioritized)

Since the procedure in Step Three involves creative thinking and "free association," it becomes necessary to structure the information developed in Step Three. Such structuring, or prioritizing, of the information about job demands is the purpose of Step Four.

Step Four involves a forced-choice quantification procedure, in which you begin with the many job features, or demands, that you wrote in Step Three and estimate their relative importance by making a series of judgments about them. This procedure results in a hierarchy of job demands that enables you to identify the critically important or most essential actions on the job.

Having a hierarchy, or prioritized listing, of job demands makes it far easier to evaluate candidates. Since no one can possibly satisfy every job demand placed on him or her, it is important to identify the critical demands—those that the candidate *must* meet if job performance is to be considered effective.

Having completed Steps One through Four, you will now have a document that should provide a target, or framework, for selection. The successful candidate should be able to produce the stated results (more specifically, he or she should be able to present evidence in the track record of having produced those results in the past), work in the specified job environment, and demonstrate competence in meeting the most critical job demands.

While *selection* is based on the information gathered in Steps One through Four, additional data are needed for *placement*—that is, data regarding the kinds of motivations required for worker satisfaction and effective performance in the job. Obtaining such information is the purpose of Step Five.

Step Five: Motivations

To succeed in a particular job, the worker requires *motivated* competence to cope with environmental obstacles. He or she must be able to produce certain types of efforts. Step Five is designed to help you identify the types of efforts, or motivations, most important for effective job performance and the intensity of the need for each type.

The list of motivations in Step Five has been somewhat arbitrarily limited to David McClelland's three social motives, plus two more of common interest: the need for security (the first item on the list) and the need for self-actualization (the last item on the list).

If these motivations are important for success in a particular job, then it would seem desirable to know whether a candidate has the necessary motivations. However, the objective determination of motivation is not so precise as is the objective determination of the factors defined in Steps One through Four. It is therefore not legally advisable to raise issues of motivation during the selection process. Such motivational factors are best considered during the placement process, when the candidate's or employee's livelihood is not at stake.

The Final Result

The job model that can be conveniently used by the selection official would be based on the above model-building procedure. But what would it actually look like? Figure 5 shows a form we have found useful.

(text continued page 42)

Figure 5. Job model.

Complete one form for each job.

Name of Job: _____

Salary Without Fringes: _____

Other Compensation: _____

Location of Work: _____

Title of Immediate Superior: _____

1. Principal Results

In the right-hand column below, list at least five results that a person in this job must be able to produce in order to be regarded as performing effectively. (Remember that a "result" is an objective *output*—a basic reason your organization wants the job done.)

In the left-hand column, indicate the relative importance of each result by putting a *1* next to the letter for the most vital result, a *2* next to the letter for the second most vital result, and so on down to the least vital result on the list. (For example, "*3 E*" means that E is regarded as the third most important result in this job.)

—— A. _____

—— B. _____

—— C. _____

—— D. _____

—— E. _____

—— F. _____

—— G. _____

2. Job Environment

In the space below, indicate the factors in the job setting that help or hinder a person's performance. That is, what is easy or difficult about this job?

_____

_____

_____

3. Job Demands*

Considering the results needed and the obstacles to attaining them above, what job demands ("motivated skills" or "competences" applied to overcoming the obstacles) are needed to attain these results? List up to eight below:

_____

_____

_____

_____

_____

_____

_____

_____

Score the candidate's data against these Job Demands.

_____

It *is* possible to select candidates without having a specific job model if you can carefully define the general competencies required for success in a career line or set of jobs. Chapter 9 describes how the Track Record Inquiry approach would be used in such cases. The principal and general method of TRI are the same as described here, but the way of obtaining evidence has to be more broad-gauged.

More Advanced Methods of Model Building

The job model form presented in this chapter can be used in almost any situation and has the advantage of speed and simplicity. However, there are jobs whose economic or other output is so significant that we cannot settle for the job model. Instead we need hard evidence that the actions described in the model, if performed, actually will lead to the desired results.

* Charles A. Dailey and A. M. Madsen, *How to Evaluate People in Business* (N.Y.: McGraw-Hill, 1980). Also, James L. Hayes, "The AMA Model of Worthy Performance," *Management Review*, February 1980, pp. 1–6.

Just such a problem confronted David McClelland and me when we were advising the U.S. Information Agency (USIA) about its selection system. In the article quoted below, Daniel Goleman gives a rather clear account of that project, based on McClelland's recollection. Goleman also shows the connection between the approach used with the USIA's selection problem and McClelland's ideas about the role of competency concepts in the selection process. I do not fully agree with the interpretation of "competency" that omits the environment from the job model. However, under McClelland's leadership, the competency approach promises exciting innovations in personnel selection.

The foreign service officers discussed in the Goleman article were not asked to describe their jobs or to go through the model-building process outlined earlier in this chapter. But they were asked to describe specific events in their work. This use of "critical incidents" (a very basic concept in this book) collected from superior and average performers in order to identify the realities of their work is the essential significance of the USIA project. It was this factual emphasis that led to the novel findings about foreign service work that were at such variance with official selection criteria.

COMPETENCY TESTING*

Back in the early 1970s, the United States Information Agency (USIA) had an embarrassing problem. Although the agency was supposed to represent American culture abroad, it had very few blacks, members of other minority groups, or women stationed in foreign countries. The staffs of USIA libraries and cultural missions were made up almost exclusively of white men.

It was not that blacks and other minorities weren't applying for the jobs. But by the time 20,000 applicants a year had been screened by the standard aptitude tests given by the agency, there were few among the several hundred top scorers who were called back for more detailed interviewing. The problem was the aptitude tests, which measured general intelligence, English usage, and background knowledge of history and government. An internal State Department study had found that scoring very well or merely average on the test bore no relationship to how USIA officers actually performed on the job overseas. On the basis of questionable criteria, the agency was turning down otherwise talented

* From *Psychology Today*, January 1981.

candidates in the first screening—among them, many women and minority members.

Seeking more sophisticated and less restrictive methods of selection, the USIA (since renamed the U.S. International Communications Agency) called in Harvard professor David C. McClelland, an eminent psychologist known for his research on power and achievement motives. Through personality tests, McClelland had identified a pattern of attitudes and habits associated with high achievers. He had given training workshops, both in the United States and abroad, for people interested in acquiring those qualities.

As McClelland recalls it, a high-ranking USIA official happened to attend one of his workshops and concluded that the same general approach might help solve the agency's selection dilemma. He posed McClelland a challenge: could he identify the motives, attitudes, and habits of outstanding USIA officers and, after identifying "the right stuff," develop specific criteria that could be used instead of the aptitude tests in choosing new officers for the agency?

The first foray into what McClelland now calls competence assessment ended in disappointment, but it laid the groundwork for a bold new approach to personnel screening and training. Competency testing, as McClelland defines it, assumes that standardized tests of intelligence and aptitude are crude instruments that may be irrelevant to real-life success. Dozens of organizations have adopted McClelland's alternative—competence assessment—with the help of McBer, a Boston-based consulting firm that he set up in 1970. McBer lists among its clients the State Department, the U.S. Army and Navy, Anheuser Busch, General Electric, General Mills, Honeywell, Owens-Illinois, and Twentieth-Century Fox.

But is competence testing just another of the smoothly packaged, quicky cures for personnel problems sold by management consultants in recent years—this one with the added cachet of a Harvard professor? To examine the method—and the evidence of its effectiveness—I talked with McClelland, his associates at McBer, and some of the people in the organizations that hired them. Which brings us back to the USIA's plea for help.

McClelland started by asking the USIA's personnel director and a few other top agency managers to nominate "water walkers," people who were so outstanding it seemed they could do no wrong. They were also asked to list another group of officers who simply did their jobs well enough not to get fired. To find out what the water walkers did that was different from what the mediocre performers were doing, McClelland and a colleague, psychologist Charles Dailey, went globe trotting to talk with each nominee.

"We developed an intensive interviewing technique," McClelland recalls. "Our idea was that in order to discover competencies, ideally we'd be like flies on the wall, watching these guys perform every day. Since that wasn't practical, we decided to make them give us detailed, blow-by-blow accounts of certain critical incidents. We were like investigative reporters. We got accounts from 50 people of three episodes in which they had done their jobs very well and three in which they had flubbed. It was always harder for them to remember the flubs. When they came up with an episode, we'd walk them through it, demanding very specific details: what was the date, where were you, who else was there, what did you say, and so on.

"Once we had this mass of what we called behavioral event interviews, we analyzed them very carefully and asked ourselves what competencies these stars had shown that the other people failed to show. We were able to distill a distinct set of competencies which set them apart.

"For example, one of the competencies was social sensitivity. A typical problem that cultural-affairs officers get into overseas is that there are directives from Washington saying, for example, that you must show such and such a film. Now, if they're in, say, North Africa, they know damn well that if they show that film the place will be burned down the next day. A Washington politician thinks it's great, but the locals will find it offensive. What they have to figure out, then, is how to show the film so that they can tell Washington that they did and yet not offend anyone in the country.

"The water walkers came up with the solution of screening it when nobody could come. In other words, they had the social sensitivity to know how the people in the country would react and also knew how to handle it back home.

"This example also points to another competence we have identified: political judgment. It's a sort of political savvy that working in a bureaucracy demands. You have to be able to maneuver within a set of regulations and directives, balancing what the home office requires and what the reality in the field will allow. You've got to know what you can do and what you can't get away with."

4

The Candidate's
Right to Know

The trend in employment jurisprudence is to treat people as
adults, rather than as "applicants" or "employees." Such treatment would go far toward reducing the most abrasive conditions
that lead to the excessive litigation now bedeviling corporate legal,
industrial relations, and personnel departments. What does this
"adult treatment" imply for the hiring (and promotion) process?

In this chapter we will examine the hiring and promotion
process as a "fair hearing." This phrase is chosen for its legal
connotations but is not to be applied literally. In fact, our intent is
to move away from the excessive legalism we see in employer-
employee relations. The way to do this is to honor the *intent* of our
legal traditions but not get entangled in legal machinery.

The intent of a court of law is to get at the truth through rules of
evidence and testimony that are known to both parties. The "applicant" is not to be treated as one accused, who has to prove his or
her innocence to be hired, and least of all as a party to a contro-
versy. However, while there is no adversary proceeding in a hiring
or promotion interview, there are two "sides," in the sense that
there are arguments for and against any person's candidacy.

What are the candidate's rights, and how can they be safe-
guarded through the procedure followed in the Track Record Inquiry? They include, in my opinion, the right

- To know what the job is.
- To know how to apply for it.

- To know the criteria by which candidates will be evaluated.
- To understand the nature of the TRI itself, including the role of the interviewer.

The Job Model and Accountabilities

At the start of the selection process, the TRI interviewer will have to orient the candidate to the TRI approach. This orientation can, in fact, be accomplished by showing the candidate the job model. *Why not?*

But one might ask, What if the model includes some of the difficult—and even impossible—features of the working environment? The answer: Show the candidate the realities of the job, warts and all. This is not only fair, but it also establishes an immediate norm of candor that will prevent many of the deceptions used by both sides in interviewing.

Figure 6 shows the form the interviewer often uses in companies that have a TRI system. Some seasoned interviewers literally show the candidate the form, since it provides a visual orientation to what is to come.

Instead of starting with the "Nice day, isn't it?" kind of rapport-building and general small talk before getting down to business, the TRI interviewer starts right in by saying, "Now, this is the kind of interview we do here, using this form. See, across the top we list the areas of accountability. I will come back to them in a minute. I am going to be very interested to learn about your background in regard to each kind of accountability. Then we get into some of the obstacles you have run into in your experience." The interviewer can in this way run through the nature of the TRI so that the candidate knows what is coming. Isn't this more adult than the traditional small talk? It seems to me more natural, as well as being a time-saver.

The interviewer may think that candidates will regard the explanation of a simple form as a bit "Mickey Mouse." But having considered the anxieties and uncertainties about hiring or promotion of a very large number of executives and managers, I can

Figure 6. Form for recording TR interview notes.

On this row, record the goal, using a descriptive phrase such as "Attain sales increase of 20 percent."

On these rows, record the candidate's reasons for expecting to be successful in attaining each of the goals.

On these rows, record notes as to examples or other strong evidence the candidate offers to back up these reasons. Continue on the back of the form if necessary.

On these rows, record major obstacles the candidate sees to attaining each of these goals.

On these rows, record notes as to similar obstacles the candidate has met in the past.

Goal A   Goal B   Goal C   Goal D   Goal E

assure you that a simple preview of what is to come and how decisions will be reached is appreciated.

Continuing to work from the job model in orienting the candidate, the TRI interviewer returns to the accountabilities and explains them briefly. Then the interviewer might pause and ask, "Any questions about any of these?" If there are none, the inquiry can proceed.

The TRI interviewer should not over-explain the accountabilities. This suggestion not only speeds up the TRI but also follows the nature of the TRI interviewer's *role*. That role is to shift the burden of candidacy off the interviewer's own shoulders and onto the candidates'. I have seen many interviewers, in trying to be compassionate, overdo the explanation and succeed only in appearing condescending. The most important point is to make the inquiry process *easier* than the traditional interviewer's role was. If a candidate contends that he or she understands the accountabilities but actually does not, that is the candidate's problem. In fact, such a situation is not a bad way to verify the candidate's claims to have had relevant experience.

Explaining the TRI

At this point in the TRI interview, we have only introduced the job model; we have not yet explained the TRI approach itself. An explanation I have used sounds in brief like this:

In this inquiry into your track record, I want to hear about the subject on which you are the world's leading expert—your own history!

Start out by listing the successes you have had that are relevant to each of these accountabilities. I will have some questions to ask about each, so that I can understand how things have gone when you had the chance to operate at your best.

As to the jobs or projects that didn't go so well, you don't have to volunteer such things. We don't ask people to testify against themselves. We do want to know what has been hard about your career—where the obstacles have been.

We have had some candidates who pretend it has all been smooth sailing, with no big obstacles. That may be true. But in all frankness, we have no way of knowing how such a candidate would perform if faced by really serious challenges.

The *interviewer's* role in the TRI process can be explained in terms of stages. In the first stage, the interviewer has the role of helping any candidate present his or her best case for the job. This does not mean the interviewer "sides" with the candidate. The interviewer represents the potential employer or boss at all stages. But in the first stage, the interviewer has as yet no "pros" or "cons" to consider. The candidate should build a strong "pro" case. It is the employer's problem to know what to believe about that case and how strongly to credit it.

The *candidate's* role in the process is to advocate his or her own candidacy. As Hillel said: "If I be not for myself, who will be?"

It is not unusual for some candidates to regard these stated roles for the interviewer and the candidate with some skepticism—until the subsequent line of questioning validates the interviewer's claims. Many candidates, however, become rather enthusiastic—if not yet quite knowing how to proceed—about the recommendation that they should be "for themselves."

They later learn, however, that the process is tough-minded and demanding. It is hard, for example, to present evidence and credible data about oneself. What has been transferred—from the interviewer to the candidate—is a burden. The interviewer has a lighter load in no longer having to ask clever questions and extract information the candidate may not care to reveal; the candidate, in turn, assumes that load.

Explaining the Rules of Evidence

In asking what the candidate has accomplished and what obstacles have been faced, the interviewer is in fact looking for evidence. Only clues will be forthcoming in the first round of questioning, but the candidate needs some forewarning so that he or she can understand the kind of process that takes place in TRI.

The interviewer may say, "We are not interested in your impressions about yourself but only in the facts of your career. That is, the strongest case for your candidacy will be factual evidence. By 'evidence' I mean primarily examples of your work given in enough detail that others here, and I, can understand what you did and how you went about it."

Here are some general rules of credibility that can be applied to the information a candidate presents:

- Examples of work are more convincing than generalities.
- The facts of a candidate's track record—the who, what, where, when, how, and how well—are much more credible than unsupported conclusions.
- Examples containing names, places, dates, and other specifics are the most credible kind of facts.
- Ratings received or other such testimonials offered by the candidate are not of interest. Facts will be verified but—as for ratings from previous employers—the TRI process will rate the candidate's track record here and now.
- A candidate's actions speak louder than psychological traits.
- The candidate's actions can be better understood if he or she also helps the interviewer understand the situations in which those actions took place.

To sum up, you might say to a candidate, "The easiest way to do well in the TRI is simply to tell what happened in your previous jobs. Give me a complete story, and we'll get along fine."

At this point, keep in mind that this chapter alone does not describe the entire TRI concept. (In fact, examples of track records have not even been presented yet.) This chapter discusses only one feature of the TRI approach—its use as a tool for giving candidates a "fair hearing" during the selection process.

How Decisions Are Reached

In explaining the evaluation process to the candidate, you can—if you are performing the combined role of interviewer and judge—simply say something like this:

I appreciate the effort you've made and will study the information you have given me. I will try to match it against the job requirements, and if the match is closer than the other candidates', we will make an offer.

For your part, having seen the job model, you should carefully consider your candidacy. Is the job that has been described to you what you really want to do? It's up to you to decide whether your own interests match up with the realities of this job.

If a committee or other person will review the track record data, this would be the time to explain this to the candidate. They, too, will decide by matching the candidate's track record with the job and comparing that match-up with the match-up of other candidates' track records.

One question that often arises with respect to the selection process: Should it be legally possible for candidates disappointed by the final outcome to examine records of the judges' deliberations and see how they did match up? By analogy with the jury process, I would say *no*. The candidate has had an open and fair hearing if you have followed the procedure outlined in this chapter and in the following one. Having had an excellent opportunity to present his or her track record, the candidate has in fact already been shown more fairness than has traditionally been offered through impressionistic interviewing. He or she has been able to make the strongest case favoring candidacy that is consistent with the facts. To go further than this is to invade the sanctity of the "jury box" and destroy its usefulness.

Candidates could nit-pick at semantics and quarrel with ground rules, such as "Recent track records are ordinarily considered more relevant than older records." One bypassed candidate might say that his or her record five years ago was really more important; another, bypassed for the same position, might argue for the principle of emphasizing the recent record. Better to avoid such discussions. TRI is not a "test" to be discussed, as an exam is reviewed in class.

The above remarks do not fully describe how decisions are reached, but only the explanation that can practically be offered to candidates. The issue of judging track records is itself complex enough that a later chapter will be devoted to it.

Preparation for TRI

Before the inquiry is begun, the candidate should have a reasonable opportunity to prepare. One cannot suddenly confront a person with such a question as "Where were you on the night of January 16, 1979?" The legal phrase is "proper groundwork." What is proper groundwork for TRI?

Presenting the track record is primarily a question of memory. The candidate has the facts of the track record in his or her memory but cannot quickly present them—not without some "warm-up" for the task and some note-taking. For lower-echelon jobs, this preparation requires only an application blank. For higher-level jobs, it requires more detailed notes. The reason for this difference lies in the time period to be reviewed. The principle is:

The higher the level of the job, the longer the track record that must be reviewed.

Application Blank. In general, the application blank can serve as a warm-up for the Track Record Inquiry. The process is as follows: The candidate completes the application blank. The job model is then explained. The candidate reviews the application and marks the sections—especially the jobs—that are pertinent to each part of the job model. The nurturant interviewer may think it unfair that the candidate may not be able to find parts of the job history that are relevant to the job model, but the TRI interviewer should not consider that his or her own problem. It is certainly the candidate's. Having tried to identify parts of the job or other history that are relevant to the job model, the candidate can "signal when ready," and the interviewer can proceed with the inquiry outlined in the next chapter.

Longer Advance Preparation. For higher-level jobs, the candidate might be allowed more time to dig into the past. He or she could be advised to prepare the day before—a preparation that might consist of compiling a detailed job history with notes to refresh the candidate's memory as to who the boss was, where the job was located, or what the main duties were. These notes are only to assist the candidate and do not become part of the TRI.

Equality of Treatment. Everyone who is candidate for the same job should receive an equal opportunity to prepare for and understand the TRI. In some Equal Employment Opportunity–sensitive situations, I would go so far as to make a tape cassette of the orientation to TRI and present it to all candidates.

Objections to the TRI Approach

It would be wise, in some cases, to permit the candidate to register objections before the TRI begins. This could be done by repeating the intention of the method and asking for feedback:

In this approach to assessment, we give you a chance to present the track record as you see it. Most people consider that about as fair as you can get. What is your opinion?

Of all the candidates appraised in this way, 95 percent have agreed that the system is seemingly fair. Some of the other 5 percent reserve judgment about the "higher-ups" or others who will review the data or have some skepticism that their record will be considered even if they present it.

However, I have run into some amusing—and slightly appalling—objections from the occasional litigious candidate. One said that it was the professional interviewer's job to know the candidate's track record—not the *candidate's* job to present it! Some candidates for promotion held that the *company* should already know their track record; it was unfair that they, the candidates, should have to present it. And many candidates subscribe to an American norm that it is bad form to present one's assets in a favorable light.

In the government, many earnest persons who have long been schooled in the civil service system believe they should be given an examination and be promoted for their knowledge and experience. That such a test has never been devised does not concern them; that is the problem of the authorities. They do insist, however, that they be examined with a paper-and-pencil test. Volunteering information about their own performance is distinctly at variance with the civil service system, as they see it.

Perhaps the hardest candidates of all to deal with are those who are favored under existing systems of social merit or seniority. Many feel, with some reason, that their opportunities are maximized if they are judged for their "merit" or seniority; they will lose only if judged for achievement and career struggles, as they will be in the TRI system. ("Merit," you will recall, refers to the social status system and its criteria.) The candidate for an executive position who looks like the whisky ad's "man of distinction" has done very well in the past when judged by the standards of the public that responds to these ads; why should he want to be judged for his track record instead?

As for seniority, it is customary to attribute this emphasis to unions. But in fact, many managers believe they know more after ten years' experience than they did after five. This is the thinking of résumé-writers; they firmly believe their formal credentials prove what they can do. The track record, however, is far from a résumé.

While 95 percent of the candidates appraised under this system initially agree that it provides a fair hearing, what happens later— when they find out they did not make it? At this later point, the above objections may be raised. The only protection for the TRI interviewer is to get agreement in principle before applying the method in practice, rather than discussing the rules of the game with those who have already lost it.

5

The Candidate
as Self-Advocate

An ancient legal precept states that a person has the right to defend himself or herself in court, facing the accusers. Although seeking a job or promotion is not an adversary proceeding, certainly there are two sides ("go" or "no-go"), and there is much at stake, as in the court of law. The emotional reactions of a candidate who did not—or feels he or she did not—receive a fair hearing cannot be ignored in employment jurisprudence.

It seems fair, as in court, to allow job candidates to speak for themselves. Many candidates have the following attitudes and would express them if they were able to speak out forthrightly:

- "I feel qualified for this job."
- "Give me the chance to show why this is true."
- "Here are the reasons it *is* true."

If this hearing is not granted, grievances build; some of them mushroom into litigation. Or the grievances do not reach litigation but take the form of cynicism and suppressed anger among the "also-rans."

The aim of this chapter is to show how a self-advocacy system provides a healthy outlet for the natural demand that we all have: to be given a fair hearing from the "powers that be."

"Self-advocacy" is the right of the candidate to volunteer information and have it seriously considered. This includes information about background and especially about the track record of past accomplishments. For such volunteering to mean anything to the interviewer, it must be in the framework of the job model and in a form that the interviewer can readily evaluate. The preceding chapters explained what this demands in the way of orientation and advance explanations to the candidate.

The great advantage to the company in providing such a fair hearing lies in the burden's being shifted away from the interviewer and onto the candidate. It is much easier for the candidate to search the "memory banks" and bring out helpful data than for the interviewer to guess what is in those memory banks. Traditional interviewer training assumed that this is what the interviewer should do. This unreasonable expectation may have contributed greatly to the validity problems of interviewing. It was just too hard to do.

A second advantage to the company lies in the legal security of dealing with data that the person volunteers. This resembles the courtroom rules that deny the attorney the right to ask "leading questions" under certain conditions. However, the jury may consider data that are *volunteered* by the witness.

These advantages of the self-advocacy approach have long been appreciated by seasoned interviewers, who ask "open-ended" questions rather than "closed" questions. For example:

- "Tell me about your last job. What was hard about it?" is open-ended.
- "Was your last job hard?" is closed.

The first question (or request) cannot be answered with a yes or no, while the second one can be answered with either and thereby "close off" the discussion.

In these ways, the candidate is encouraged to tell his or her story. A narrative account is ordinarily given in enough detail to betray the candidate's inconsistencies and allow the interviewer to estimate credibility. Glossy, abbreviated summaries raise questions of credibility. But this gets ahead of *our* story in this chapter.

Other advantages of asking the candidate for a narrative account ("Tell me what happened during the last year you worked at General Motors") include: revealing the candidate's work setting— which may or may not have resembled the environment in the job being sought; revealing the causes of successes and failures, rather than merely asserting that there were some ups and downs; showing the candidate's modus operandi, or style, and not just describing successes and failures.

Can such a self-advocacy procedure be used with all kinds of candidates? Or are there some kinds who cannot present themselves in this manner? Fundamentally, the same procedure is followed with everyone applying for a key job. If they cannot be assertive enough to handle the Track Record Inquiry (the "TRI"), they probably cannot be assertive enough for a key job.

However, we will describe variations on the procedure (all within the same overall framework of the Track Record Inquiry) that can accommodate the differing capacities of less-articulate and lower-echelon candidates as well as the more communicative and assertive higher-echelon ones. We will begin by describing the basic TRI system—the principles of which can be applied to candidates at all levels. The final part of the chapter will discuss the additional considerations involved in the more advanced type of TRI used with applicants for higher-level positions.

The Basic TRI System

As discussed in the previous chapter, the first step in conducting the TRI can be showing the candidate the goals listed on the form for recording TR interview notes (see Chapter 4, Figure 6) and explaining that these are the results for which the candidate would be held accountable in this job. The form then guides the structure of the TRI.

For the first goal (A) defined in the Job Model, the candidate is asked to give reasons why we should consider him or her likely to be successful in producing this result. Some candidates are momentarily taken aback with such questions. There is a norm in the United States (and perhaps elsewhere) that stating one's good points is immodest and not done by the "good ol' boys." Many women have traditionally been trained to admit freely how much they have to learn but to glance modestly downward when asked about their chances to succeed.

Although it is not the track record interviewer's role to give a short assertiveness training course, the interviewer might offer examples of how some candidates deal with the request: "Some people mention experiences they have had; others mention their education and training. I'd just like to know what *you* think." This might help a hesitant candidate get started.

Another comment that might prompt a candidate is: "A lot of people think they will be misunderstood if they brag a little bit; it's OK—provided you can back it up." Still another comment might be "Why don't you think back to the reasons why you applied for this job. If you hadn't thought you could do the job, it would be a waste of time to take it if offered. So let's see if you can reconstruct what you might have been thinking."

The modest, hesitant, or inarticulate candidate can be given some initial suggestions like those above. But if this does not work for getting the candidate to volunteer reasons for optimism about goal A, I would not make a determined effort to "pull" information out regarding the other goals. In fact, that would be condescending. Let the candidate struggle with the question. To do *more* would be to return to the excessively difficult role of the traditional interviewer. Moreover, it would provide unequal treatment for different candidates. The unequal treatment would not only pose Equal Employment Opportunity (EEO) problems but it would also make the resulting data not comparable from one candidate to the next.

The interviewer continues on, asking for reasons the candidate expects to be successful in attaining goals B, C, D, and E as shown in Figure 6 (see Chapter 4). A few notes for each goal are sufficient. The purpose of these notes is to set up the next stage of the inquiry; they are not part of the TRI results that will be evaluated.

Steps in Brief. At this point, the TRI interviewer can explain to the candidate the role the candidate is expected to play in the track record interview:

Step 1. In this first step, the candidate has just been asked to volunteer one or more reasons for expecting to be successful in attaining each of the job goals.

Step 2. The candidate will then be asked to *amplify* the most important of these reasons by giving a "critical incident" or some other information from the track record to concretely illustrate his or her reasons for expecting to be successful.

Step 3. The candidate will be asked to describe what might be the greatest obstacle he or she would have to overcome to be successful in attaining each job goal.

Step 4. The candidate will be asked to *amplify* the most important of these anticipated obstacles by giving a critical incident or some other information from the track record, again to concretely illustrate the reservations expressed in Step 3.

The purpose of the interviewer's providing the candidate with the above outline is to help the candidate anticipate what is coming so he or she can more easily provide the data to complete the interview.

Candidate Response to the Basic TRI System. After the interview is begun and explained as described above, most candidates seem gratified to understand the structure of the interview, feeling that it means there will be no tricks, gimmicks, or unpleasant surprises.

An occasional candidate will find the track record way of thinking about job qualifications not especially congenial, however. Here are typical personality or attitudinal problems characteristic of such "uncongenial cases":

• A CPA felt that his work did not break down into episodes such as critical incidents, so he simply could not illustrate the reasons for his assertion that he was "intelligent enough to carry out the job duties" in order to accomplish goals A, B, C, etc. Instead, he was firmly convinced that having the CPA (and a good business education before that) and an excellent résumé with two years' experience ("As you can no doubt see on my résumé")— these should be enough to illustrate his reasons for expecting competence in performing the job as a whole rather than in attaining each specific goal in it.

• A corporate attorney was unable to recall specific cases in his practice that would show he could deal with antitrust and EEO problems. When given an opportunity to search into his files for such cases, he still could not provide examples of his approach or effectiveness. I finally asked him, "Why do you expect us to take your effectiveness on faith?"

• A "fast track" young advertising executive offered to present testimonial letters supporting each job goal: "Wouldn't that be better proof than anything *I* could say?" The answer was *no*.

Although cases such as these would more properly be handled using advanced TRI, which is discussed in the last section of the chapter, they aptly illustrate a particular attitude toward the track record approach that interviewers occasionally encounter.

In contrast, there were instances of candidates who never felt they had a fair hearing with other assessment systems but did feel they were being given a full hearing with this one:

• A housewife returning to the job market was allowed to volunteer any reasons she wanted for expecting to be able to work successfully in the customer complaint department, even though she had never actually held such a job. She came up with examples from her experience as a *consumer* that proved more convincing to the head of the customer complaint department than the more direct experiences offered by other candidates who had held titles such as "customer relations specialist."

• A Spanish-speaking candidate (knowing some but not a great deal of English) expressed tremendous gratification at being permitted to volunteer data in his own way rather than (as he had expected) having to fit himself into the personnel system in which he would not show a good fit.

• An engineer wanting to step up into management had hesitated to apply for a promotion. He had never "managed," as he saw it. But when pushed to give more specific reasons for expecting to be successful in attaining the goals in the job of research and development manager, he was—to his own surprise—able to see that he had already been "managing" himself, his time, his budget, and his relationships with others.

Amplifying Reasons for Expecting Success

Thus far we have been discussing the first step in the basic version of TRI—asking the candidate for reasons why he or she might expect to successfully attain each goal and then giving a bird's-eye view of the four steps to be followed in the TRI system. The second of these steps is to have the candidate "amplify" the reasons into solid evidence by citing some "critical incidents."

I find that most candidates can understand the concept of "critical incidents." The interviewer begins by explaining to the candidate what such an incident is:

A critical incident is a particular example of very effective performance on your part—including the specific details of what actually happened. These include what the situation was, where it happened, who was there, what you and others were trying to do, what obstacles to success you encountered, how you solved your problems, and why you succeeded.

The interviewer can then give the candidate some examples of critical incidents. The "Travel Agency Case" shown here is one of my favorite illustrations of what is and what is not a critical incident. Most candidates readily understand why the second version of the travel agency personnel file entry qualifies as a critical incident.

TRAVEL AGENCY CASE

What Is a Critical Incident?

Compare the following two versions of entries made in the personnel file of Ms. Julie Wilson by her supervisor and use the questions below to decide which version meets the criteria for being considered a "critical incident."

Version 1

I have had to fire Ms. Wilson, my newest travel agent. After eight weeks on this job, she is still just too weak in customer relations for what I need here. That'll teach me to hire anyone under 25. Typical Bennington girl. If I had hired a Lexington resident it would have been different. I warned her, and the date is in the files. The first thing was in March: She forgot a woman's request for special dietary meals on the plane. The latest thing is no follow-up. Today's is the last incident I'll put up with. You want an entry in the files? There it is, "April 3, 1980—bad customer relations."

Version 2

March 18, 1980. Mrs. DeBono, passenger on a round-trip, first class PAN AM flight to Caracas, requested vegetarian meals. Julie made a notation to request them but did not. When asked about it, she said, "It just slipped my mind." I warned her that all specific passenger requests must be noted and filled. Failure to do so twice is sufficient grounds for dismissal.

April 3, 1980. Mr. Ronald Charles lost his bag on Delta flight 305, which we had reserved. He arrived home in Lexington at 2 A.M. and did not properly request the airline to find his bag. He called Julie at 9 A.M. very upset. She was overheard to say, "We don't do that. You will just have to go to the airlines." Mr. Charles called me to say that he couldn't understand why our agent could not at least have told him the number to call at Delta and the procedure to follow. He was very angry about the "indifference."

Criteria for a Critical Incident

Does the information given specify
 who was involved?
 what happened and what the problem was?
 when the incident took place?
 where it happened?
 how the person tried to solve the problem?
 how it turned out (a tangible business result—good
  or bad)?

Having helped the candidate understand the concept of a critical incident, the interviewer can say, "Tell me about a time when you did something on the job that leads you to offer this reason for optimism that you can attain goal A." The key phrase is "time when." Left unspoken is the implication that if the person cannot offer such an example, why should the interviewer believe it ever happened? I have had people tell me that they have very good "analytical ability." When asked to specify why they think so— such as a time when they showed such ability—they would say something like:

- "I tested high in school."
- "I saw my assessment report at the company."

- "I received a very high score in problem solving at the assessment center."
- "I got good grades in science."

None of these is acceptable as direct evidence of analytical ability on a job. None provides evidence that the candidate—regardless of whatever analytical ability he or she might actually possess—has been able to *use* it effectively at work.

Candidates have also told me they possess "creative ability." But they see it as a general characteristic of theirs, which cannot be demonstrated in any specific way. In that case, I wonder aloud why they believe it will be shown in this particular job. Pressed further, such a candidate may finally say, "Well, I don't know how I can *prove* I have creativity; I've just always had it." Or even: "My mother told me so."

There are, however, claims to some types of skills and abilities that a candidate cannot be expected to readily amplify through critical incidents. A good example would be a candidate's claim to understand neuro-anatomy. In that case, acceptable evidence would have to be:

- "I made an A in all three neural anatomy courses I took."
- "Here is the textbook I wrote on neuro-anatomy."
- "Here is a copy of my Nobel prize acceptance speech, given in Stockholm last year."

(However, the last would, come to think of it, represent a reasonably convincing critical incident!)

Obstacles
The third step in the basic version of the TRI probes for evidence on the negative side, illustrating what the candidate cannot do. However, we cannot really ask a person to testify against himself or herself. Nor are we seeking such negative information in a devious way when we ask

- "What might you have to overcome in order to attain this goal?"
- "What reasons have you for thinking this goal might be especially hard?"

Inexperienced candidates may not recognize what makes a goal hard. Thus the reasons offered during the third step of the TRI might be revealing in themselves. Typical responses of an inexperienced person (if the goal is indeed hard for many people) might be: "It doesn't sound hard to me at all," or, "I have found I can succeed at anything I really put my mind to." In other words, the candidate is either being evasive (while knowing well that the goal is hard) or may be too innocent to recognize that many people do fail to attain such a goal.

Seasoned candidates may answer the question about obstacles in a way that does not point to their own history. For example, "In police work, it is always harder to find the drug pusher than the drug user. You just have to get more help from the FBI on tracing the connections in your town." Or, in sales, the seasoned candidate might say, "It is really hard to stay within discount policy with this kind of merchandise." These might be knowledgeable answers to the question about obstacles, but they do not lead us back to the track record. This is no reason for discrediting the candidate, but it is reason for pushing further to obtain concrete examples from the track record illustrating why a goal looks hard.

Amplifying Obstacles
The amplification of a reason why a goal might be hard is the reverse of the amplification of reasons for confidence (discussed in Step 2). The interviewer might say something like this to the candidate:

If you will recall, a critical incident is an example of very effective performance on your part. Now I am very interested in your thinking back in your job history to times when you ran into a lot of difficulty in carrying out your work on tasks similar to those required to attain this goal. I am not interested in your personal shortcomings, but rather I want to find out what kinds of obstacles you have met in the past—and what you did about them.

Here the TRI may make its most important contribution. The full understanding of a person's track record is not going to come to the interviewer out of a mere "laundry list" of successes. This may, indeed, be one of the important failures of MBO: Lists of objectives met or missed cannot really tell us much about cause and effect structures within a person's performance track record. Indeed, there are abundant historical examples of repeated failures in people that were the most positive kinds of failures—General Grant in the west, for example, or Douglas MacArthur retreating masterfully in the Pacific campaigns. The interviewer can honestly assure the candidate, however, that what is being sought is not a list of failures, since the TRI is not designed to compute the candidate's batting average. The intention is to obtain enough detailed accounts of obstacles faced to provide an understanding of how the individual sets goals (perhaps they are impossibly high) or responds when others assign him or her very hard tasks.

Among the probing questions that are useful in getting a candidate to recall past obstacles that lead to some doubts about the job presently in question would be:

- "What was the hardest job you ever had? Why? Can you give me an example of a time you ran up against that particular hardship?
- "Who was the most difficult or unreasonable boss you ever had? How did you find it possible to cope with that job, anyway?"
- "Are there some barriers to success that you have found you repeatedly have to struggle against over a long period of time or in many different situations?"

Then the interviewer comes back and relates these answers to the difficulty of the particular goal by asking, once more, for a critical incident that illustrates the relevant obstacles the candidate has faced.

Advanced TRI

The basic strategy discussed above is also followed with advanced, top management, able, articulate, or self-confident candidates. The only distinctions lie in the amount of detail that is required and therefore in the amount of preparation and the time needed for TRI. More detail is required because there is more risk involved with these higher-level positions. Examples of the ways in which more detail is required are:

- The TRI covers more years.
- More job elements may be specified.
- The candidate is permitted to amplify his or her oral comments by providing additional written examples.

There is no difference in the interviewer's role with such a candidate. However, I have known some interviewers who treat higher-level candidates with deference and feel it is somehow less necessary to confront them with a demand for evidence than when the candidates are lower-level or less assertive.

Sociologically, it is easy to understand this deference. The interviewer may be afraid because of the candidate's high status, or the candidate may be so assertive as to seem intimidating. It is impossible, however, to justify the gentler treatment of a candidate who is better-equipped for confrontation. Only a bully would feel justified in treating the young and disadvantaged sternly merely because they cannot assert or defend themselves as well.

The simplest advice is to treat both levels of candidates alike. But if there is to be a difference, it must be in the direction of more demanding treatment of the high-status and able candidates, if only because they are being considered for jobs that pose a higher risk for the organization (if the wrong candidate is selected). Rarely have I met a qualified senior candidate who did not respect the probing search for evidence.

It is on just this point—the probing search for evidence—that many professional interviewers fail in assessing higher-level candidates: They stop too soon and settle for impressions. One reviewer of my 1971 book on assessment expressed surprise that there are still people left who really want to know the details of another person's life history. That is, in an era of 30-second television spot advertisements and a general decline of attention, are there many who want to probe for the detail necessary to reduce the risk of making a poor appointment?

Here is the most curious fact of all in the selection of high-level talent. Immense sums are being paid to recruiting or search firms for *finding* such candidates, out of all proportion to the investment in *evaluating* those candidates. I do not believe that the 33 percent rule (charging one-third of the first year's salary) is unreasonable to fill a position. What *is* utterly unreasonable is that, of this 33 percent charge, most of it (say, 32 percent) goes for the mechanics of the search and for an impressionistic interview, while the tiniest fragment (say, 1 percent) goes for a thorough evaluation comparable to that described in this chapter.

Let us be specific. The search fee for an executive who is to be paid $100,000 may total $33,000. That seems reasonable because the risks of hiring a poor executive are several multiples of that $100,000. But what is *unreasonable* is that the investment in the detailed, evidence-producing evaluation of the finalists is trivial in comparison. You have only to consider the scant back-up documentation offered in such cases to know this. The report submitted on a candidate who has not been thoroughly evaluated (as described in this chapter) may total only a few sketchy typewritten pages. A track record evaluation, in contrast, will cover five years and include ten pages of critical incidents and five pages of yearly reports. This would not include the objective history and the interviewer notes.

What often obscures this lack of evaluation is the search client's preference for receiving an oral report or at most a one-page memorandum. There is no reason the final recommendation from a TRI cannot be as condensed. But to make that final one-page recommendation without first developing thorough supporting documentation is to raise serious questions as to the basis for the recommendation. The same executive who settles for personnel triviality would not accept such triviality in taking other business risks.

6

The Track Record
Versus Other Data

The essential method involved in the TRI is to look at the candidate's past history to see what evidence is relevant to the present decision. But there are several versions of "the past." The purpose of this chapter is to clarify the similarities and differences between various concepts of the candidate's track record, in order to be very clear about what kind of evidence is solid enough to use in the TRI. We will compare the TR with:

- The application blank.
- The résumé.
- The interviewer's *impression* of the TR.

Application Blanks

There are two universal methods of selection: All employers (in firms with more than 50 employees) use at least a rudimentary interview and an application blank. This is true if we include the résumé as a form of application blank. (However, there are enough differences that we will discuss the résumé in a separate section below.)

What does the application blank do that so many employers would insist on having it, and why is it insufficient as a measure of the candidate's track record?

Apparent Advantages of Application Blanks

First, let's acknowledge the application blank's great assets. Its universal usage is probably due to two factors: its seeming objectivity, its value in providing a factual framework for further inquiry in the interview, its apparent justice (in letting a person say why he or she should be considered for a job), and its validity.

Objectivity. Objectivity is a slippery term, as you will discover if you take a closer look at it. Why is it more "objective" to ask a candidate to answer *yes* or *no* questions (since these broad categories often distort the truth) than open-ended questions? The originally presumed "objectivity" of the application blank proved somewhat less than that under the onslaught of Equal Employment Opportunity (EEO) challenges. Many "objective" questions—religion, marital status, arrest record—were challenged as prejudicial and removed from application forms by corporations aware of their liabilities under EEO law. What remained after the surgery were items that were both objective and job-relevant—especially with respect to the job history.

As for the "objectivity" of the *yes* or *no* format of the traditional application blank, this is surely the wrong word. It is not more objective to answer yes, no, or in a multiple-choice format: It is simply more convenient and standardized. It is convenient for the candidate, the interviewer, and the statistician or computer analyst. The candidate can quickly zip through a categorically organized application blank; it would be more trouble to organize written answers. The interviewer can in a similar fashion glance through a categorically organized blank much faster than if he or she had to review written essays. As for the statisticians or computer analysts who process application blank data—they would be helpless if faced with essays or open-ended questionnaire data.

We will nevertheless follow conventional usage and refer to the standardized, categorically organized application blank as "objective," although it is no more so than "objective" personality inventories and interest tests.

Framework for Further Inquiry. If the claim of objectivity for the traditional application blank was spurious, it is at least easy to see how it provides a factual framework for the further steps to be taken in assessment. The interviewer knows what to say ("Oh, I see you are from General Motors") and what to elaborate upon ("Tell me more about the year you took off and 'bummed' around Europe").

The application blank's value as a means of providing a framework is well known to personnel interviewers, but less well appreciated is the preparation the blank requires on the part of the candidate. In the TRI, the preparation of the candidate is far more important than in traditional assessment. The candidate needs help in searching his or her memory banks, time to do it, and perhaps leisure to pursue it. Completing an application blank meets those needs.

Justice. We have already discussed the candidate's rights in the assessment situation: to present his or her reasons for feeling qualified for the job. From that standpoint, it is as important to ask the questions in an objective application that everyone *expects* to be asked, as to meet the company's needs for that information. Pursuing this line of reasoning further, it is equally important to ask the candidate at the end of the application blank: *"Have you anything else you want to add?"* But this is the very purpose of TRI itself: It permits the candidate to provide a major elaboration of his or her track record.

Validity. The research-proven validity of objective biographical data (or "biodata") has surprised many of us who were accustomed to regarding application blank data as trivia. Indeed, in one assessment program (at the University of Michigan in the 1950s), the candidate's application blank (the old federal form 57) was regarded as a mere credential—a near-zero baseline of information above which the "truly scientific" measures would prove their superior validity. But time—and curious investigators such as William Buel* and William Owens**—have elevated the status of biographical data. Surprisingly high validities have been reported—note the results from Buel's research paper shown in Figures 7 and 8.

---

* William Buel, "Alternative to Testing," *Personnel Journal,* May 1972, pp. 336–341.
** William Owens, "Background Data," in *Handbook of Industrial and Organizational Psychology* (Chicago: Rand McNally, 1976).

Figure 7. Biographical scores and performance ratings for 122 engineering salespersons.

| | Below-Average Performance Group | | Above-Average Performance Group | |
| | | | | |
Biographical Score Range	Percent of Group In or Above Score Range		Percent of Group In or Above Score Range	Biographical Score Range
25–26		••	3	25–26
23–24		•••	8	23–24
21–22	5	•••|••••••••••••	27	21–22
19–20	16	••••••••|••••••••••••••••	52	19–20
17–18	39	••••••••••••••••|•••••••••	67	17–18
15–16	63	••••••••••••••••|•••••••••••••	90	15–16
13–14	82	••••••••••••••|••••••	100	13–14
11–12	95	•••••••••		11–12
9–10	100	•••		9–10

Figure 8. Biographical scores and performance ratings for 100 production supervisors.

| | Below-Average Performance Group | | Above-Average Performance Group | |
| | | | | |
Biographical Score Range	Percent of Group In or Above Score Range		Percent of Group In or Above Score Range	Biographical Score Range
20–21		•••	6	20–21
18–19	4	••|••••••••	22	18–19
16–17	16	••••••|•••••••••	37	16–17
14–15	37	••••••••••|•••••••••••••	63	14–15
12–13	59	•••••••••••|••••••••••	83	12–13
10–11	76	••••••••|••••••••	98	10–11
8–9	90	•••••••|•	100	8–9
6–7	98	••••		6–7
4–5	100	•		4–5

Source (Figures 7 and 8): W. D. Buel, *Personnel Journal*, May 1972.

However, traditional personnel researchers have not quite known what to do with the biodata method, and it does raise questions about discrimination. For example, consider the religious issues raised by a biodata finding that being brought up in an upper-class Jewish home is a good predictor of success in the arts or medicine. Would we use such a fact to select candidates? Clearly, biodata validity may be great, but the legal and ethical issues it raises are not yet fully understood.

Here we will be content with merely acknowledging biodata's validity and understanding its implications for the validity and proper use of TRI. The essential principle, as William Buel put it, is that "past behavior and experience predict future behavior, that past learning, acquired habits, and previous accomplishments carry over into the future." This is demonstrated in many contexts—including selection—such as in banking, as shown in the data on mortgage delinquency given in Figure 9. In fact, the entire insurance industry is based on Buel's principle!

How well does the biodata predictability principle apply in selection? Buel reports, "Biographical scores are related to job performance, both with respect to score magnitude and numbers of individuals in particular score ranges." These findings have been demonstrated in regard to selecting engineering salespersons (see Figure 7), production supervisors (see Figure 8), field representatives (for an organization offering financial and credit reference services), foreign nationals engaged in sales, research investigators, various line and sales managers, and middle managers (for a state government's division of employment security). These are only samples of the ongoing work, illustrating that the problem with biodata is not its validity but its other drawbacks, cited below. At the same time, the underlying principle—the track record principle stated by Buel—is basic to the TRI as well as to objective biodata.

If TRI can solve the problems of objective biodata, then what validity can we hope for? Experiments have been conducted that support the hope that TRI will break through the same low ceilings on validity that objective biodata has. These experiments will be summarized in a later chapter. Here we continue to explore the

Figure 9. Mortgage application blank (biodata) scores and delinquency status of 100 mortgagees.

Biodata Score	Percent Delinquent Accounts in or above Score Range		Percent Nondelinquent Accounts in or above Score Range	
Over 70	0%		+ + + + + + + +	16%
65–69	0		+ + + + + +	28
60–64	4	00	+ + + +	36
55–59	12	0000	+ + + + + +	48
50–54	24	000000	+ + + + + + + +	64
45–49	32	0000	+ + + +	72
40–44	46	0000000	+ + + +	80
35–39	56	00000	+ + + + + + +	94
30–34	72	00000000	+ + +	100
25–29	82	00000		100
20–24	94	000000		100
15–19	98	00		100
10–14	100	0		100

Source: Used with permission of W. D. Buel.

similarities and differences between objective biodata and track record data.

Let us look at the following step-by-step procedure that Buel has used to achieve advanced levels of validity with objective biodata:

1. Administration of a biographical questionnaire (such as the sample research questionnaire shown in Figure 10) to applicants whose job performance is known.
2. Collection of that job performance data—such as ratings, productivity, and tenure.
3. Analysis of the responses to each questionnaire item to differentiate the high from the low performers (for example, perhaps the military service item—No. 9 in Buel's questionnaire—separates the two groups).
4. Preparation of a shortened questionnaire and scoring key that includes only the legally permissible items found valid above and a scoring key to be used in future selection.

(text continued page 81)

Figure 10. Sample biographical questionnaire (for research purposes only).

This questionnaire is to be answered by checking the alternative to each question which is most descriptive of you or your situation. As a ground rule, *please check only one answer* to each question. Multiple checks on questions where only one check is required will confound our analysis.

The sample question below indicates how you are to answer.

How old were you when you started work at this organization?

a.___18 or younger   d.___23 to 24
b._✓_19 to 20   e.___25 or older
c.___21 to 22

Notice that the person answering the question above was 19 to 20 years old at the time of employment with this organization and therefore made a check mark in the space in front of "19 to 20." As you proceed through the following pages, answer each question as accurately as possible. Before you begin completing it, please fill in the information requested below:

Name _____ Age ____

Location _____ Today's Date _____

Your Job Title _____

1. What is your height?
   a.___5'4" and under   d.___5'11" to 6'1"
   b.___5'5" to 5'7"   e.___6'2" to 6'4"
   c.___5'8" to 5'10"   f.___6'4" or over

2. What is your weight?
   a.___120 pounds or less   e.___171 to 190 pounds
   b.___121 to 130 pounds   f.___191 to 210 pounds
   c.___131 to 150 pounds   g.___211 pounds or over
   d.___151 to 170 pounds

3. How old were you when you joined this organization?
   a.___20 or younger   g.___31 to 32
   b.___21 to 22   h.___33 to 34
   c.___23 to 24   i.___35 to 36
   d.___25 to 26   j.___37 to 38
   e.___27 to 28   k.___39 to 40
   f.___29 to 30   l.___41 or over

Source: W. D. Buel, personal communication, 1972.

4. How many brothers do you have or did you have? (Check greatest number.)

   a.___none
   b.___1
   c.___2

   d.___3
   e.___4
   f.___5 or more

5. How many sisters do you have or did you have?

   a.___none
   b.___1
   c.___2

   d.___3
   e.___4
   f.___5 or more

6. Which child were you in your family?

   a.___only child
   b.___oldest
   c.___next to oldest
   d.___youngest

   e.___next to youngest
   f.___one of twins
   g.___other

7. What was your marital status at the time you joined this organization?

   a.___single
   b.___married, no children
   c.___married, one or more children

   d.___widowed
   e.___separated or divorced

8. How old were you when you were married (the first time if remarried)?

   a.___not married
   b.___less than 18 years old
   c.___18 to 19 years old
   d.___20 to 21 years old
   e.___22 to 23 years old

   f.___24 to 25 years old
   g.___26 to 27 years old
   h.___28 to 29 years old
   i.___30 or over

9. If you were in the service prior to joining this organization, which service was it?

   a.___Army
   b.___Navy
   c.___Marines
   d.___Air Force

   e.___Coast Guard
   f.___other
   g.___I was not in the armed forces.

10. What was the highest rank you held in the armed forces prior to joining this organization?

   a.___Private or Apprentice Seaman
   b.___Noncommissioned or Petty Officer

   c.___Warrant or Flight Officer
   d.___Commissioned Officer
   e.___I was not in the armed forces.

11. How many persons (adults and children) other than yourself were directly dependent upon you for their upkeep when you joined this organization?
    a.___none
    b.___1
    c.___2
    d.___3
    e.___4
    f.___5
    g.___6
    h.___7
    i.___8
    j.___9 or more

12. The high school which you attended for the longest period of time was:
    a.___public
    b.___parochial
    c.___private
    d.___military
    e.___trade or vocational
    f.___did not attend high school

13. How many times did you change schools before you were 18 years of age—other than by graduation?
    a.___Never
    b.___1 to 2 times
    c.___3 to 5 times
    d.___6 or more times
    e.___I can't remember

14. My major subject in high school was:
    a.___academic–college preparatory
    b.___agricultural
    c.___business or commercial
    d.___fine arts or music
    e.___trade or industrial
    f.___other
    g.___did not attend high school

15. To how many student offices were you elected in high school?
    a.___0
    b.___1
    c.___2 or 3
    d.___4 or more
    e.___did not attend high school

16. What was your grade-point average in all your major courses up to the point at which you quit high school or graduated?
    a.___A minus or better
    b.___B plus
    c.___B
    d.___B minus
    e.___C plus or lower
    f.___did not attend high school

17. Which of the following high school courses was easiest for you?
    a.___physical science, chemistry, physics, mathematics
    b.___natural science, biology, zoology
    c.___history, economics, civics
    d.___commercial courses, bookkeeping, typing
    e.___shop courses
    f.___English, literature, humanities
    g.___art, music
    h.___home economics

18. During your high school days, in which of the following did you participate most? (Check as many as apply.)
    a.___sand-lot games
    b.___Scouts, 4-H Clubs, FFA, YMCA or YWCA
    c.___student government
    d.___student publications
    e.___science clubs
    f.___social clubs
    g.___music organizations
    h.___cheerleader
    i.___honorary societies
    j.___I worked or studied and did not participate
    k.___did not attend high school
    l.___other (please specify)
    _____
    _____

19. What was the last grade you completed prior to joining this organization?
    a.___10 or below
    b.___11
    c.___12
    d.___freshman in college–13
    e.___sophomore in college–14
    f.___junior in college–15
    g.___senior in college–16
    h.___partial master's degree–16 +
    i.___master's degree–17
    j.___above master's degree–17 +

20. The number of students in the college in which you received most of your undergraduate training was:
    a.___less than 100
    b.___101 to 300
    c.___301 to 500
    d.___501 to 700
    e.___701 to 1,000
    f.___1,001 to 2,000
    g.___2,001 to 5,000
    h.___5,001 to 10,000
    i.___more than 10,000
    j.___did not attend college

21. In college, how many times did you change your major before you selected the one in which you graduated?
    a.___never
    b.___once
    c.___twice
    d.___three or more times
    e.___did not attend college

22. What was the college subject which you took and liked the most?
    a.___architecture
    b.___biological sciences or agriculture
    c.___business administration or economics
    d.___education
    e.___engineering, physical science, or mathematics
    f.___English or literature
    g.___fine arts or music
    h.___foreign language
    i.___journalism or speech
    j.___physical education
    k.___psychology or social sciences
    l.___religion or philosophy
    m.___none of these
    n.___did not attend college

23. What portion of your expenses did you earn during your college career?

    a.___none
    b.___1% to 10%
    c.___11% to 20%
    d.___21% to 30%
    e.___31% to 40%
    f.___41% to 50%

    g.___51% to 60%
    h.___61% to 70%
    i.___71% to 80%
    j.___81% to 90%
    k.___91% to 100%
    l.___did not attend college

24. During your last year in school (grammar school, high school, or college) how much time did you average on part-time work per week?

    a.___none
    b.___1 to 5 hours
    c.___6 to 10 hours
    d.___11 to 15 hours

    e.___16 to 20 hours
    f.___21 to 25 hours
    g.___26 to 30 hours
    h.___more than 30 hours

25. Prior to age 18, what one part of the newspaper did you read regularly?

    a.___editorials
    b.___features
    c.___financial page
    d.___news
    e.___syndicated columns
    f.___the funnies

    g.___the sports page
    h.___want ads
    i.___all of these
    j.___something else
    k.___did not read a paper

26. How many times did you and/or your family move your residence from one town to another before you were 18 years of age?

    a.___never
    b.___1 time
    c.___2 times
    d.___3 times
    e.___4 times

    f.___5 times
    g.___6 times
    h.___7 times
    i.___8 times
    j.___9 or more times

27. Prior to age 18, about how many hours a week, both in and out of school, did you spend on athletics?

    a.___none
    b.___1 to 4
    c.___5 to 9

    d.___10 to 14
    e.___15 or more

28. Prior to age 18, I usually spent my summers:

    a.___attending summer school
    b.___going to camp
    c.___studying for the next school year
    d.___taking life easy

    e.___taking a vacation alone
    f.___vacationing with family
    g.___working on a farm
    h.___working in town
    i.___doing something else

29. In what size city did you spend the largest portion of your time to age 18?

    a.___rural or country
    b.___2,500 to 25,000
    c.___25,001 to 50,000
    d.___50,001 to 100,000

    e.___100,001 to 250,000
    f.___250,001 or more
    g.___suburb of large city

30. The community in which you spent most of your time prior to age 18 could best be described as:

    a.___a mining town
    b.___an industrial city depending upon very few activities
    c.___an industrial city with diversified activities
    d.___a rural or farming community

    e.___a small town with practically no industries
    f.___a suburb of a large town or city
    g.___something else

31. How old were you when you became completely independent of financial assistance from your family?

    a.___14 or younger
    b.___15 to 16
    c.___17 to 18
    d.___19 to 20
    e.___21 to 22
    f.___23 to 24

    g.___25 to 26
    h.___27 to 28
    i.___29 or older
    j.___I am still not financially independent

32. How old were you when you got your first part-time job?

    a.___14 or under
    b.___15
    c.___16
    d.___17
    e.___18
    f.___19

    g.___20
    h.___21
    i.___22
    j.___23
    k.___24
    l.___25 or more

33. For how many companies did you work prior to joining this organization?

    a.___1
    b.___2
    c.___3
    d.___4
    e.___5

    f.___6
    g.___7
    h.___8
    i.___9 or more

34. What was the average length of time you spent on your jobs prior to joining this organization?

a.____had no previous jobs   g.____5 years

b.____less than 1 year   h.____6 years

c.____1 year   i.____7 years

d.____2 years   j.____8 years

e.____3 years   k.____9 years

f.____4 years   l.____10 years plus

35. What was the nature of the job you held immediately before joining this organization?

a.____sales   g.____factory work

b.____owner of own business   h.____store employee

c.____management other than   i.____labor

    ownership   j.____other (please specify)

d.____office work   _____

e.____trades   _____

f.____farm work   k.____I had no previous jobs.

---

5. Administration of the new questionnaire to a group not previously measured, to see if the total score (the sum of the items a particular person answers in the predicted direction) is valid.

6. Installation of the shortened questionnaire as a validated selection tool for that particular organization and job.

As to the problem of discrimination, the answer Buel found in the 1972 procedure outlined above (he has devised additional refinements since that date) was to validate separately for race and sex. Only if a biodata inventory was proved valid for a particular group could it be appropriately used.

Problems of Using Application Blanks

From the TRI standpoint, the valid results described above for biodata are most encouraging. Biodata and TRI are both historical methods. What supports the validity of the first encourages us about the validity of the second. But can we, in the design of TRI, overcome the limitations of standardized application blanks? What are those problems and limitations?

First, the biodata can be *too* historical. That is, there is a difference between a past event that can never recur and one that can. Growing up in a stable home may be a good predictor of job tenure, but the early home data are in a book forever closed: There is nothing whatsoever a person who "failed" that item can do to alter the unchangeable historical facts. It does not seem fair to doom the child of a broken home throughout life. Let us take, for contrast, an item such as "Was in the top half of the sales force in volume of sales achieved." This event, too, is historical; but something *like it* could conceivably happen again. The person who failed in the past to demonstrate above average sales performance still has a chance to perform better.

The second problem is that biodata can measure events that are beyond the control of the person. Again, growing up in a stable home may be a valid predictor of job performance, but the individual did little to bring about the events that we call a "stable home life." Therefore, is it fair to credit such a candidate with the personal qualities that produce a stable home life? If there are in fact no personal qualities present in the candidate today that are indicated by the historical event, then the predictive validity of that event may be a statistical accident that merely reflects some other more truly predictive event we have yet to discover.

The third, and most serious, problem with the application blank is that it describes social merit better than it does performance. We discussed that problem earlier, in the context of what is legal under EEO law. The problem of social merit, however, is much larger than the problem of discrimination. It involves the issue of whether we will try to orient the selection process toward solving the massive problem of industrial productivity in the United States or toward such lesser—but more convenient—goals as cost, bureaucratic simplicity, and protecting the personnel department from criticism.

The arguments favoring biodata are implied rather than stated by those who lean heavily on such background facts as a basis for selection, but in essence they are as follows:

- Application blanks are very inexpensive.
- They standardize the hiring process and screen out atypical

persons so that hundreds of candidates do not have to be interviewed for each position.

• The personnel department will not be criticized for hiring a person with conventional social merit, even if that person later turns out to be a poor or unreliable performer.

Among these arguments, we focus here on social merit. In Buel's sample biographical questionnaire (discussed earlier and shown in Figure 10), can be found the following instances of social merit: height, weight, seniority (items 1, 2, and 3), marital status (item 7), military service (item 9), military rank (item 10), and so on. Most of the items will be found to have a social status value. (This is not a criticism of Buel's research; in 1972 he was only using items that were then often used in social science research and in personnel departments for selection.)

These social merit items could be considered evidence of past achievement, but every such item is also evidence of past privilege. Consider, for example, the Harvard graduate. Here is a credential suggesting educational attainment. Whether or not this is true, this credential also proves an original *admission*—a privilege awarded. Someone thought this candidate should be granted a Harvard education. But isn't that evidence that the candidate had merit? To answer such a question, you would have to find out why people are admitted to Harvard University. You would discover that the admission decision is based on facts that are themselves indicators of earlier privilege in life—not necessarily "family connections" but certainly the privilege of life in a superior learning environment.

The foregoing is not an argument against regarding a Harvard degree as an indication of merit. The proposition is that such a fact reflects some *unknown mix* of social and performance merit.

Fundamentally, then, much of biodata (and therefore the content of even the sketchiest application blank) is a record of past privilege. Let's consider some more specific examples of how employment officials use different kinds of biodata, since some of them pose more problems of recognizing true, or performance, merit than do others.

Job History. If we ask a candidate to list the jobs held and their duration and locations, can we get an objective measure of "past experience"? Objective, yes—but what is being measured? A person who has been manager of an engineering department was evidently considered qualified by his or her company at one time. This is not, however, evidence of *performance*. The promotion or appointment may have been for seniority or on political grounds. But suppose that person was manager for five years. Does "five years" really measure "experience" and, by implication, performance? Job history would therefore appear to be a very weak measure of performance:

- Tenure on a job proves *at most* that the person performed, or was thought to perform, just well enough to avoid getting fired.

Suppose we further ask the candidate to list the salaries paid, and we observe that increases of substantial size were awarded, until the candidate's annual income is now well above the standard paid to such engineers. Does *this* prove performance merit? Such "market value" of a person proves nothing unless you know how the compensation is managed in that company. People are given salaries and increases for many reasons other than performance. It is quite possible that the compensation was merely for holding the job, not for the performance. Salary would therefore appear to be a very weak measure of performance:

- Salary indicates the person's tenure, the value of the position held, and the reward system of the corporation more than it indicates the performance level of the individual.

Educational History. Usually the application blank will also request the candidate's highest degree and other facts of his or her educational history, even grades in some cases. The final degree awarded, however, only proves that the student performed well enough not to be dismissed. For that reason, more careful employers often inquire into grades. Here, the ice is thinner than is commonly known. Of 36 occupations surveyed in one research study, the final report showed that performance in only one (research engineering) was satistically related to grades. That is, college grades do not predict job performance, as a rule. What they do predict is admission to graduate or medical school—if only because those admission committees review the grades.

Hence, degrees and grades have a weak relevance to occupational success in that in a "credentials society" (which ours is), a person can get advanced only if a committee will do it. When the realities beneath the paper are examined objectively, the procedures are discovered to be a sham. For example, one study of physician performance showed that objective performance of physicians (as indicated by such criteria as patient recovery rates and excellence in surgery) had nothing to do with their medical school grades. Education (in terms of either quantity or grades) appears to provide only a weak measure of performance:

- Credentials or grades prove how likely a person is to advance within the educational hierarchy. They show little, if anything, about performance levels in most jobs.

Military History. Patriotic employers may wish to afford privileges to those who have served their country; in following this policy, they would be in the good company of the civil service regulations followed by the government itself. However, we should be as clear as possible about the meaning of a military record: Promotions reflect the extent to which a soldier survived in battle long enough to be promoted for seniority; awards reflect the military system for recognizing merit; less-than-honorable discharges reflect the operation of the military courts.

Of these three kinds of data that you might find requested on an application blank, only the awards given in battle seem to have any semblance of merit. If you believe peacetime rank does measure merit, you should know the frequency with which high-ranking officers (who attained their promotions during peacetime) are removed during battle; the military promotion system is a most dubious measure of excellence in an officer, at least with respect to his combat worthiness. And before accepting a veteran's military discharge credentials, you should really know more about military justice.

A case can be made for giving a candidate credit for a military record: A high-ranking officer is accustomed to command. If this is relevant to a particular position, I would consider it. The strongest case would be for the military "battle ribbons" and honors. The weakest cases would be in the areas of military justice and tenure (years served in the armed forces)—as measures of *performance*. If an employer wants to give privileges to those who have been exposed to military risk as a patriotic policy, this is another issue—but this policy has nothing to do with the issue of validity.

Physical Health. I am aware of no validity studies that relate health data to industrial performance. Such data concern problems of insurance premiums and health costs and are outside the scope of selection based on performance.

Emotional Health. The reliability of judgments about "mental health" or "emotional fitness" is so poor that most corporations make no attempt to cover this on an application blank. Occasionally, a sales executive remarks that it is urgent to screen out the "alcoholics." Such screening is theoretically possible, but practically speaking it is not feasible in an application blank.

Implications of Application Blanks for the TRI
In summary, the implications of application blanks for the TRI process are as follows:

1. The validity of biodata encourages the study of the TRI's validity.
2. To avoid the problem of crediting or discrediting events long past, the TRI should be directed toward events that are recent enough to have some relevance to the present. For example, why not follow a ten-year "statute of limitations" for executive jobs, five years for middle management, and one or two years for entry-level jobs?
3. The TRI should inquire into events under the person's control or at least under his or her partial influence. It should not ask about privileges awarded as much as about how those privileges were *earned*. It should not ask for mere job history but should also focus on job performance.

4. Every question asked in TRI should be framed for its proper intent—to find high performers, not to strengthen the system of social status.
5. Measures of tenure and salary levels must be rejected as indicators of performance.
6. In view of the problems associated with educational, military, or health history, it is suggested they be excluded, except for entry-level positions or for persons for whom there are special arguments that they be included (such as a 20-year military careerist seeking a position in industry).

Résumés

The résumé, too, is a miniature history. Can it reveal the candidate's track record? If not, what can it reveal that we need to know in selection?

On the surface, the résumé appears to provide the candidate the opportunity to volunteer the data that he or she wants considered. What, then, are the differences between it and the TRI? What, in essence, are the omissions?

A résumé shows the privileges a person has had—the opportunities awarded—not the performance in those positions. The résumé is therefore incomplete until the interviewer has "cross-examined" the candidate about what it means.

Thus far, our view of the résumé agrees with prevailing practices among those who have had experience recruiting or evaluating key personnel. Where TRI differs from these standard practices is summed up in the preceding chapters, especially in regard to the rules of evidence and the necessity of being sure that the candidate also knows those rules. At most, the résumé is the basis for asking questions about a candidate's history. Then, in TRI, we go on to ask the candidate to amplify the résumé, providing historical examples along lines that are relevant to the job model.

It should be added that amplification, in the form of specific critical incidents and a broad narrative history of the candidate's career, is done differently in the TRI than is standard among personnel interviewers and executive recruiters.

Interviewer Impressions Versus the TR

Many interviewers use the data described—application blanks and résumés—and ask the candidate to amplify those data so that he or she can be "matched" against the job sought. The interrogation may well unfold then somewhat as prescribed in the preceding chapter. Yet in the end, the interviewer may fail to function as TRI prescribes because he or she rates an *impression* rather than evaluates evidence.

Aside from the legal liabilities of being unable to document the basis for the job offer (or non-offer), what is wrong with an impression? Is it not far more flexible than writing things down? Isn't the documented interview likely to become bogged down with note-taking, and aren't we creating new and gargantuan problems with the paper mill? There are, in fact, three fundamental problems with basing selection decisions on impressions.

The first thing wrong with an impression is that it cannot be checked with a peer or explained to a disappointed candidate. A physician who wants to discuss a case with a colleague must be able to say what facts were found; with only impressions, there is nothing to discuss.

A second shortcoming of the impression is in learning. With only impressions to guide the selection process, the interviewer can understand nothing about the reasons for his or her mistakes in hiring or promoting. Let us say that the interviewer chooses an engineer to head up the sales department. Later the employee turns out badly. Reflecting back on the reasons for the choice—to avoid making the same error again—the interviewer needs to consider a more extensive explanation than that the candidate was "an engineer." This may not be the cue that was overlooked or badly used in predicting his success in heading up the sales department. If there are no notes, if there is nothing more than an impression in the interviewer's head at the moment of decision, there is no basis for learning.

The third problem with impressions is that forming them makes the selection responsibility so frightening. The interviewer has the awesome duty of judging another person and controlling his or her destiny. The duty is awesome in part because it is vague and ambiguous.

Simplifying the Task. The problems of the paper mill and the objections to note-taking by boards or interviewers are greatly simplified by passing the burden to the candidate. After the candidate has named the examples that support his or her case in regard to a particular part of the job, the interviewer can say, "Please write me a memorandum describing that example as fully as you can— but limit it to two pages."

The Resulting Documentation. What the candidate writes or the interviewer's own notes on the examples and history offered during TRI can be kept in the files for the period of legal liability in discrimination suits or—more importantly for the vast majority of cases—until the interviewer can get feedback on that candidate's job performance.

The total TR, then, contains three kinds of history:

- The objective history—including the application blank, résumé, and factual credentials. Here the focus is on the facts of a career rather than on what they mean or the effects of what was done.
- Work samples, such as critical incidents. Here the focus is on particular, or crucial, events within a career described in enough detail that the quality of performance can be estimated.
- Comprehensive history, such as is covered in a yearly report. Here the scope is very broad and includes facts and events occurring or sequenced over a long enough time period that trends can be seen, with the relationships among events and facts being as important as the facts and events themselves.

These three perspectives on work history are mutually complementary. What is missed in the objective history is revealed in the work samples. What the work samples cannot show is revealed in the broad, or comprehensive, history.

In other words, the objective history can report what the candidate did (the jobs held, for example), but not how *well* he or she did it. The work samples, or critical incidents, show that excellence of performance. The critical incidents volunteered during TRI do not show whether they are *typical*, however. Acts of heroism, for example, may be performed by very ordinary people under unusual emergency conditions; that hero may never again display similar courage or initiative. The broad history provides the long-term context into which the critical incidents fit and makes it apparent whether a particular success or failure is part of a consistent career pattern, or whether it was a single "flash in the pan."

For these reasons, at the end of the TRI, I encourage the candidate to write or dictate a three-page comprehensive career history covering the last decade (for executives), three to five years (for middle managers), or one to two years (for entry-level workers). It should not only contain facts but also show *how* successes were attained and *why* there were disappointments.

7

The Track Record
Versus Assessment
Centers and Testing

In this chapter, we will compare the track record with two nonhistorical forms of assessment—assessment centers and testing. By "assessment center" will be meant a procedure in which:

- Candidates perform simulated tasks—tasks resembling those they would perform if hired or promoted to the position in question.
- Their performance is observed and rated—usually by company officials higher in rank than the position they seek.

By "testing" will be meant use of a standardized set of questions, usually presented in printed form, that can be scored for right or wrong answers. The term "test" excludes personality inventories and interest questionnaires, since they cannot have right or wrong answers. This use of the term "test" is narrower than that found in some legislation or executive orders of the federal government. (The legislative language, using "test" to refer to any selection procedure, blurs over some critically important distinctions.)

Assessment Centers

The essential idea of the assessment center is that of simulation, and in this regard it resembles some tests. However, a group of observers is commonly used rather than one test administrator and scorer.

Historically, the assessment center is directly descended from the OSS (of World War II) to the military field exercise as a way of proving who can perform under battle conditions. Battle-like stress would appear essential for producing a realistic assessment. The OSS, trying to identify good spies, put candidates under life-like stress and observed their reactions and performance excellence.

At the University of Michigan in the late 1940s the first large-scale research program to investigate the validity of various selection procedures included some such simulation. I remember going through that Michigan assessment and being subjected to a number of stresses, including one of having to give a speech on five minutes' notice to a senior group of professors.

Following the assessment research program at Michigan, which was a research success in that the predictions made during the program were kept "locked up" and then checked for accuracy five years later, the next well-known rigorous application of simulation was at the American Telephone and Telegraph Company. There again, the predictions were locked up and verified several years later. This verification indicated the validity of assessment centers, but it is worth noting in passing that the use of life history or track record data also proved very promising in that AT&T program.

Following the AT&T success, assessment centers spread throughout American industry and in Western Europe. Among the factors leading to that acceptance were not only the validity shown but also the participation of line management as observers rating the candidates' performance.

At Ford Motor Company, I had the chance to validate the assessment center ratings by comparing them with the track records of 24 candidates for foreman and middle management positions. Unfortunately, the assessment center ratings were of "traits" rather than performance results. While I do not think track record data are the best way to evaluate traits, we nevertheless estimated the traits used at Ford and obtained results similar to those of their assessment center for foremen but not for middle management.

Unfortunately, the Ford instance is the only one known to me in which the outcomes of the two systems of assessment were compared. Notice, however, that in attempting to validate the assessment center ratings, the managers of the Ford assessment center regarded track record data as the *criteria*. In other words, data about the everyday working performance of a candidate tended to be accepted as the facts against which to validate other assessment procedures (including not only assessment centers but also testing).

Similarities Between TRI and Assessment Centers. TRI and assessment centers do have points of similarity: Both should be based on a carefully developed job model, if possible. If this is not feasible, they should be based on an explicit "action-model" (see Chapters 9 and 10), not on traits. (Unfortunately, many assessment centers do seem to appraise traits rather than actions, but this is not an inherent limitation of the assessment center approach.)

The assessment center is supposed to enable management to observe performance like the future performance that will be required on the job; it is a simulation approach. TRI, too, is oriented toward the documentation of on-the-job performance, but it is an approach that focuses on actual past performance.

Differences Between TRI and Assessment Centers. The assessment center enables direct observations of performance to be made, while the track record interview depends on the reconstruction performance based on the candidate's memory. This direct observation is a major advantage of the assessment center. There are, however, compensating advantages for TRI:

- The candidate can be questioned during TRI about some necessary competences that cannot be simulated in the assessment center. For example, we may need an executive who can raise capital.
- There is an enormous difference in the time-span. Using TRI, the candidate can be questioned about the past ten years. The assessment center lasts, at most, three days.
- TRI can be used to evaluate the candidate, without the results being affected by his or her appearance, age, speech, skin color, sex, or race (as in the assessment center, where direct observations are made). Such biases are excluded from TRI if the "panel" method is used (in which evaluators review written track records).

The inability of the assessment center to set up situations that are analogous to certain parts of the job creates some highly undesirable possibilities. For example, a sales manager was the top performer among ten districts for five years in a row. Yet the choice among sales managers for the next national sales director was to be made on the basis of an assessment center. The sales managers with the top seven performance records were assessed. The traits appraised gave the highest score to a manager whose performance happened to be about average. Should this score, based on three days' observation, be given more weight than the five-year track record? If so, the main reason for the job—to obtain sales results—would be overruled.

Viewing candidates as they work at the simulated tasks in the assessment center is an asset, but at the same time it makes the center vulnerable. Line managers often enjoy participating in a center, but can we say that they are not swayed by their prejudices about candidate appearance, sex, race, or age or by any other subjective bias?

Complementary Contributions of the Assessment Center. The assessment center is here to stay, at least for lower-echelon positions. It needs several improvements, however, according to the analysis here. It needs more objectivity, and it needs to be validated more often against performance results on the job rather than against trait measures, popularity measures (such as whether a manager gets promoted), or tenure. Using the assessment center in conjunction with TRI would appear to be a way of strengthening it at its points of weakness.

Testing

Paper-and-pencil testing went into decline, perhaps unfairly, following the challenges on Equal Employment Opportunity grounds. The test was more objective than many other selection procedures, if by "objectivity" we mean freedom from scoring bias. The problem was, according to David McClelland, the leading advocate of competency measurement, that the qualities tested for are not those required for success in the real world.

We especially found this to be true of the testing program (discussed in Chapter 3) used by the U.S. Department of State to select foreign service officers. In designing a more valid testing program, McClelland actually traveled abroad to collect occurrences in which what foreign service officers did had an impact on the foreign relations of the United States. No one had done this before; hence, the old tests used to select foreign service officers were not validated against events in the real world but only—as testers are usually satisfied to do—against other tests and convenient measurements.

But suppose we did construct paper-and-pencil tests to measure qualities required for success in the real world. Industrial users of tests ought to consider the inherent limitations such procedures have for personnel selection. These are:

- An apparent low ceiling on the tests' validity (some authorities have estimated that ceiling to be about .50).
- The tests are *on paper*. They measure written responses to questions, not events on a job or directly observed (as in an assessment center).
- They measure *abilities*. Even if the abilities were like those required for success on a job, the concept "ability" only refers to a fraction of what causes an event to take place. They measure effort poorly and have nothing at all to do with situations.

The last point requires clarification. If we want to predict an outcome (say, a sale), we need three kinds of information: the situation (or setting), the obstacles to making the sale, and the actions taken by the salesperson to overcome those obstacles. The concept of ability refers only to the last factor, and is at most only a part of action (the other part being effort). Perhaps the marvel is that tests do as well as they do.

Complementary Contributions of Testing. In spite of these grave doubts about whether testing can ever (or should ever) return to the preeminence it once had in personnel selection, the objectivity of test scoring is an advantage. Further, there are certain kinds of performance that appear to be well suited to being simulated on a paper-and-pencil test. These include quantitative problem solving and some verbal abilities. The ideal assessment might therefore include a few tests of numerical and verbal skills.

Using Job Models to Design a Comprehensive Assessment Program

In an earlier chapter, a project in which critical incidents were collected to construct a job model was briefly outlined. Here we will give an example of how this same method might be expanded to develop the "dimensions," or competences, that ought to be evaluated in a comprehensive program—including elements of the TRI, the assessment center, and objective tests.

Suppose you wanted, as we did, to select word processor (WP) operators. We began by collecting critical incidents. You will recall that a critical incident is a particular instance of performance—one that has an objective enough outcome to permit us to say that the performance was either effective or ineffective. To decide what elements in a job have key importance, many such incidents are collected and analyzed. Recurring dimensions of the job can then be seen, such as:

- Obstacles and other situational "field forces" that stand between the person and the outcome.
- Actions (consisting of competences or skills) taken to cope with those obstacles.
- The person's efforts or persistence in taking those actions.

On questioning a number of word processor operators and their immediate superiors to identify the job elements that had key importance, we learned that the operator who produced superior contributions to the offices where the WP unit was located was actually doing few things that resembled the duties listed in the original job description. Whereas WP operators were hired to carry out duties that resembled those of stenographers, actual instances of outstanding operator contributions turned out, in the critical incidents collected, to consist of something very different. These contributions (or failures to contribute) consisted of incidents like these:

1. The WP operator persuaded one sales manager to put his field reports on disks that would be kept for only a limited time, saving an immense paper file space.
2. The WP operator did not succeed in getting the payroll clerks to use the new equipment properly.
3. The WP operator persuaded two stenographers to accept elementary instruction in the use of the equipment so that they could "backstop" her when she was ill or take some of the overload.

Analysis of a large number of such incidents revealed that the WP operators were very often dealing with the following obstacles to maximum contribution:

- Fear of, or skepticism about, the equipment on the part of other office workers; that is, others would not get sufficiently involved.
- Inability of management to see that the added equipment would greatly increase their control over their operators.
- A common perception by many (including most of the WP operators themselves) that the equipment was a way to type something faster and more accurately, whereas its major contribution was actually in *re*-editing.

Based on these obstacles discovered in the critical incidents of WP operation, several recommendations were made for how one could identify potentially high performers. Among these were: to look for operators who had run into such obstacles before (regarding any kind of equipment, not just word processors); and to select those who showed a positive attitude toward coping with such barriers.

Analysis of the critical incidents also revealed certain competences that were required over and over again. For example, an effective WP operator was a moderately fast typist, but this competence did not distinguish the better operators. Instead, the essential competences were of these types: persuading people to enjoy the new possibilities of the equipment, training people, and helping people reorganize what they were doing to include the WP equipment.

Finally, the critical incidents showed that the best WP operators persisted over very long periods of time in persuading people to enjoy, try out, and learn how to use the equipment.

What to Assess and How to Do It

As developed through the above procedure, the list of obstacles faced and the competences and efforts to be evaluated in order to select WP operators were as follows:

- *Moderate* typing speed and accuracy (instead of superior).
- Overcoming others' fear of the equipment.
- Overcoming others' skepticism about the equipment.
- Overcoming management's "tunnel vision" about WP.
- Overcoming their own misperception of the equipment's purpose and its major assets.
- Persuasion.
- Training people to use the elementary capabilities of the WP.
- Helping people reorganize the way they were handling paper and other information so that they could utilize the main advantages of the WP.
- Patient persistence over very long periods of time in inducing people to enjoy, try out, and learn how to use the equipment.

The next step was to find the best way to assess candidates with respect to each of these items. The first item—typing speed and accuracy—was easily tested. A simulation (a role-play) was developed for overcoming fear and skepticism about equipment. Such a simulation was also devised for training people to use the elementary capabilities of the WP. The other items on the list all became features of the TRI. For example, it was decided that overcoming managers' tunnel vision could not be simulated, because it was too gradual, but a candidate could be questioned to see whether he or she had ever faced such a task in the past.

What resulted was a comprehensive selection procedure based on TRI, the assessment center, and testing. Findings from all three methods were combined to select future WP operators, and the position was successfully upgraded to its full potential—requiring a person able to ensure that an office exploited the full capacities of the new equipment.

8

The Track Record,
the Boss,
and "Gut Feel"

The oldest system of personnel selection is the most intuitive. Before there were personnel departments, the boss would hire from a "labor shape-up" or its equivalent. Production workers might be sent over from the hiring hall—ten, perhaps, in response to three new job openings. The boss would line the workers up, walk up and down, and point to "You, you, and *you*. The rest of youse, go on home." Did it ever happen this way?

Whether it did or not, there is one feature in this anecdote that is still true: the deference given by the personnel department to the final judgment of the boss. What happens to justice in a hiring or promotion system if—in spite of the efforts to inject objectivity and other elements of a fair hearing—at the very end, an intuitive choice is made by a casual or even a biased superior?

This remnant of "divine right" is sometimes rationalized as helping the chosen candidate survive. The rationalization is that, if the boss makes the final choice, he or she will feel an identification with the worker and help that person succeed. Some such rationalization is also offered by civil service tradition, in which all the candidates are objectively examined but names of the top three finalists are submitted for an intuitive final choice by top management.

In this chapter, we will examine this intuitive choice and some options for tolerating it without allowing it to destroy the selection system.

There are at least two strong reasons why the boss of tomorrow will have to become more objective in making selection judgments. One is the obvious risk of litigation that grows almost daily as more and more employees resort to legal remedies when they feel they cannot obtain just treatment through corporate decision-making machinery. The second is the overwhelming and growing demand for productivity in American corporations. This demand, if properly focused on the human resources function rather than only on buying new equipment as the route to productivity, will instigate innovations in the hiring and promotion functions.

Before discussing intuition and its role in the selection process, we must define the concept of "intuition." By intuition, I mean simply the inability to specify precisely where you got your conclusions. Intuition per se is neither good nor bad: Its effect depends entirely on the role it is allowed to play in the overall selection process.

For example, using the TRI approach, you may evaluate several critical incidents and conclude that the candidate shows initiative. Although intuition might have played a minor role in your decision—at least to the extent that you could not precisely specify what factors in the data prompted the decision—your conclusion was, in fact, based on the evidence. You might have been wrong, but you were not being intuitive.

On the other hand, you might judge a candidate without gathering any data or hearing any evidence—pulling your decision out of thin air, so to speak. In this case—while you might be right—intuition has played far too great a role for your decision to be fair.

In short, we need to distinguish between the following two forms of intuitive judgment of a job candidate:

Intuition I: Gathering data and drawing conclusions based on those data, while being unable to say on exactly what points in the data you "made up your mind."

Intuition II: Drawing conclusions without any data or without consulting the data.

We can be sympathetic with Intuition I and are not convinced that intuition in this sense is necessarily invalid. Intuition II, however, is an unfair basis for selection that has no possible validity—when used by the boss or by anyone else.

The Arguments Against Objectivity

So far, we have argued that for a fair selection system you need the most objective data you can obtain—data from assessment centers, testing, and the track record in some reasonable combination. Who could be opposed to that, and on what grounds?

- Expense. Conducting a TRI is more expensive than a brief interview. Both are more expensive than following Intuition II, described above.
- Humanity. Some people feel that there ought to be some place in selection for the "gut feel," and that trying to be objective or scientific will take even more of the warmth out of personnel work or business.
- Impossibility. This argument is put forth by those who believe that managers or others we are selecting will be successful only if they possess certain intangible qualities that are impossible to objectify.
- Trouble. It is a lot of trouble to gather data and much simpler to stick with Intuition II.
- Confidence. Many decision makers believe they have accurate decision-making ability when it comes to selecting people; some even believe they are infallible.
- Unimportance. Some managers denigrate the hiring and promotion function. They will not consider systematic and objective assessment, because they consider human resources generally—and hiring and promotion in particular—to be either insignificant or not subject to logical analysis.

The argument regarding expense is most easily refuted by data showing what it costs to replace an employee. These costs range from six months' salary on up, according to estimates I have seen. However, I remember when some colleagues and I gave one plant manager cost data on his labor turnover, in hopes of inducing him to adopt more reasonable policies. The data showed a loss of a quarter of a million dollars per year from labor turnover. He finally accepted the data but dismissed our proposal, saying, "In my experience, the soundest way to increase profits is to increase sales." He did not even want to consider labor or personnel policy.

"Gut feel" seems a more human approach—until you are the one who is victimized by someone who won't look at facts but rejects you anyway. But—on the positive side—we use "gut feel" to choose a mate: Who would want to give tests or collect a TR from someone before asking for a date? The most pleasant of our intimate human relationships are regulated by intuition. Therefore, why objectify employment? Obviously, it depends on how vital the job or the promotion is to the other person. If it is really vital, that person will resent an employer's playing dice with his or her career.

Intuition II advocates may have a favorite gimmick for divining the future—tea leaves, astrology, or an unvalidated test. Because such "gut feelers" are often oriented toward "inner qualities" that cannot be shown in observed performance, they are likely to reject the objectivity required for TRI. (This is not to dispute that there are such things as personal traits and inner qualities; the issue is whether they can be used as a basis for selecting personnel. There *is* one respect, however, in which I would agree with Intuition II. One cannot objectify—or predict—everything in the world and claim total accuracy in doing so. It might be a bit boring if we could.)

The "too-much-trouble" argument from the tired, overworked manager is the hardest one to refute. This manager may not care about trying to make a better decision and may even be disinterested in the kind of data we get in personnel selection. While it is a bit hard to imagine a manager lacking interest in the human factors of management, it is true that the kind of decision making advocated in this book is not taught in business schools. Many managers are not prepared for it because they were not educated to think about track records.

However, it would be a simple enough project to put together such courses to train managers in the track record approach. My associates and I did so at American University (with support from the School of Business) and used the course materials at Dartmouth College (with premedical students, who need to be good at judging people, of course), as well as in several overseas projects and in American corporations. These included Interstate Brands, IBM, Control Data, and some areas of the federal government. In general, the courses intrigued the participants because of the prediction tasks they were asked to perform—an approach which will be described later in this chapter.

Another argument against objectivity comes from the Intuition II manager who is convinced of his or her infallibility. Such a conviction can easily be dispelled by using the prediction tasks mentioned above. While it is possible for these managers to succeed at prediction tasks much of the time, they will quickly discover that it is not possible to make an accurate prediction in every case.

The most annoying argument against the hiring and promotion demand for objectivity is that offered by managers who ignore or denigrate the human resources area in general and the hiring and promotion problem of validity in particular. Such managers evolve through almost any area of university graduate study: They may be found in law, medicine, psychology, engineering, or history. The example below, which happens to be from the field of engineering, illustrates the disastrous consequences for personnel selection when such "tunnel vision specialists" reach a position of power.

Along the "high technology" belt (on and nearby Route 128) in Boston, there are a number of high-growth-rate companies, whose growth is attributed to a timely and ingenious product of some sort. When prosperity suddenly loomed, otherwise hard-nosed managers demanded large numbers of personnel quickly. In one such instance—which unfortunately is not rare—the company did not share its planning with the employment manager. The result was a *very* hasty expansion.

Through giant ads, candidates were invited to attend an "open house" to be held in the largest hall in a local motel—last used for a convention of door-to-door vitamin sales representatives. On the appointed evening, the hall was filled with engineers and a buzz of conversation. At a dozen desks, "interviews" were being held— each about ten minutes. This resulted in the wholesale hiring of 100 candidates, after no more than a glance at their résumés. It was a "system" devised by a top management that was indifferent to the complexity and the importance—not to say the dignity—of careful hiring.

The penalties for such tunnel vision (the top management just described was thinking only about its particular technical specialty) are harsh and expensive. They consist of prices paid later in turnover and burnout for bad choices and hasty decisions. Sooner or later, each such high-growth-rate company begins to recognize this problem—when it sees an otherwise promising expansion grind to a halt.

Training Managers to Become Objective

Earlier I referred to a course that has been developed to train managers in making objective selection decisions. It consists of a simulation of the TRI—that is, a simulation of the process of making judgments on the basis of critical incidents collected during TRI. The purpose of such training is to induce managers to base their decisions on evidence (rather than on Intuition II) and to make explicit forecasts that can be verified.

You will recall that "Intuition I" means judging a candidate on the basis of evidence but without being able to say exactly why the judgment was made; "Intuition II" means judging a candidate without any evidence at all; and "evidence" refers to observations of behavior or performance—not to feelings, impressions, or irrelevancies.

Hence, to train managers, we need to present evidence to them, let them make judgments, and give them feedback on the validity of their judgments to help them learn how to make better use of evidence when their predictions are inaccurate.

The two designs used, which are discussed below, are based on factual feedback and peer feedback.

Factual Feedback
In this design, managers were given a series of critical incidents and asked after each one to predict what the person in the incident would do. After each prediction, managers were told what the person actually did. This constituted the "feedback."

Figure 11. Increases in decision-making accuracy as the result of factual feedback.

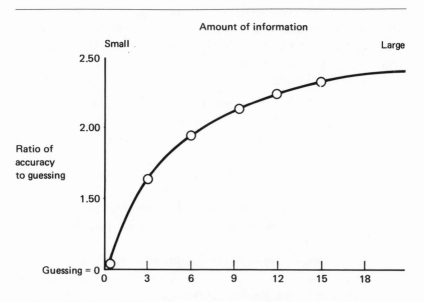

Source: Charles A. Dailey, *Assessment of Lives*. San Francisco: Jossey-Bass, 1971.

What happens in this kind of learning is that the predictive accuracy increases within each personnel case (managers become more accurate, the more critical incidents they know), and there is also an improvement (based on a modest transfer of learning) from each case to the next. The accuracy levels improve from about chance (Intuition II predictions made without any evidence) to over 75 percent. The learning profile (within cases) is shown in Figure 11.

The figure shows the results from one particular version of the training course taken by 59 middle managers from several companies, including Interstate Brands, Control Data, and IBM. Other versions of the method were used with Korean and Belgian college students, Peace Corps men and women, employment counselors, military officers, and others.

The data are based on 15 performance predictions made by 59 managers and administrators in each of six personnel cases. The cases consisted of critical incidents. The ratio of accuracy to guessing is a statistical correction to eliminate chance. The guessing level was about 33 percent accurate, so that with a large amount of information, the managers eventually achieved about a 75 percent accuracy rate (a ratio of 2.3 × 33 percent was achieved after 15 units of performance information).

Among the findings were these:

1. "Gut feel" exists. Participants in the experiments could often make valid predictions but yet be unable to say how.
2. Some participants were consistently better judges than others.
3. Validity of judgment increased with the number of critical incidents known to the participant.
4. There was a modest transfer of skill from one case to another case over the series of 12 cases (that is, during about 12 hours' training).
5. The findings were valid cross-culturally. When cases written in English were translated into French or Korean, we obtained the same learning curves.

Peer Feedback

The second source of feedback to a manager who is making impressionistic judgments without feeling accountable for them is from peers. In this method, the managers read a set of cases similar to those used in factual feedback courses. (The description of Donna Cole, shown here, is a sample of the type of cases that were used.) The manager was then asked to predict the future prospects for the person described in each case according to the instructions given in Figure 12.

Instead of confirming the manager's accuracy in predicting the future behavior of the person described in the case—as was done with the factual feedback method—the similarity of his or her predictions to those of other managers was reported. This process was done with groups of managers. After completing each case, the managers compared their total "optimism" scores for the per-

(text continued page 109)

Figure 12. Estimating potential.

INSTRUCTIONS

In considering a person's experience, we ought to look for ability wherever it is shown. There seems to be no obvious reason to limit appraisal to paid work. For that reason, the following questionnaire asks for two kinds of judgments:

- About competences shown during full-time work.
- About competences shown in home life, social life, civic affairs, and part-time work.

You will be shown a number of cases and, for each case, you will be asked to judge whether each of the ten statements below about the person described in the case is—or will be—true in the following three time periods:

Now   Check *column* (a) if you can prove that the statement is true or has been true based on evidence in the case record.

Near Future   Check *column* (b) if the record leaves the impression that the statement will become true, or remain true, during the next two years.

Eventually   Check *column* (c) if the record leaves the impression that—if conditions are very favorable for the person described—the statement will eventually become true, or—if true now—it will remain so.

Put a "0" in the column for any statement you feel is *not* true in the particular time frame. When something used to be true but no longer is, base your answer on what the evidence shows now.

EXAMPLES

	(a)	(b)	(c)

If you have read the case of an engineer who is presently unemployed but has always been employed and seems competent, you would have reason for optimism. Therefore, in response to whether the statement "Holds a job— is self-supporting" is true, you might answer: 0   √   √

If you have read the case of a student in the first year of law school who gives you the impression of having great potential ability as a lawyer, you could not check the statement "Holds a job—is self-supporting" as being true *now* (since the student has over two years of study remaining), but you might answer: 0   0   √

STATEMENTS

(a) (b) (c)

1. Essentially law-abiding—repays debts, is a good neighbor, votes, has no serious criminal convictions.   ___ ___ ___

   On this item, assume that a person is innocent and law-abiding unless the evidence shows otherwise. This is the only item for which positive evidence is not needed.

2. Conscientious worker—shows up at work on time, does not cheat on expenses, shows effort.   ___ ___ ___

   Answering affirmatively on this item does not mean that the worker is effective—only that he or she tries.

3. Holds a job—is self-supporting.   ___ ___ ___

   For this item to be answered affirmatively, the person must be holding a job at the end of the case. Housewives and others not technically employed are not credited on this item (but they may be credited under item 6, if meeting their family obligations).

4. Does a good job—gets results and is productive.   ___ ___ ___

   This item does not mean the person merely *tries*, but that he or she actually works *effectively*. Answer according to what is true whenever the person is working. (The item can therefore be answered affirmatively even if the person is not now employed.)

5. Is in line for promotion—is considered promotable by the boss or by others in authority.   ___ ___ ___

   This item does not refer to being "next in line"— having seniority. Answer this item affirmatively only if the person is now employed. For persons who are self-employed, answer affirmatively if the business or activity is likely to expand significantly due to the person's performance.

6. Is an effective family member—meets obligations to those in the household.   ___ ___ ___

   This item applies to obligations between spouses, parents and children, siblings, or friends living under the same roof.

	(a)	(b)	(c)

7. Creates or preserves jobs for others—including starting a new business or raising capital.   — — —

   This item is used for crediting entrepreneurs and employers as well as labor officials or attorneys attempting to preserve job security. Do not credit a person for merely supervising someone else.

8. Contributes to the wider community—serves on volunteer boards concerned with community welfare.   — — —

   This item does not include service on political or business boards (which is covered in item 9).

9. Holds major elective office (such as in the state legislature) or serves on a board of directors of a major civic organization or corporation.   — — —

   This item refers to *official* offices, requiring formal appointment or election.

10. Publicly advocates a point of view through writing articles or books or speaking.   — — —

    This item refers only to writing or speaking that *advocates a point of view* rather than that done for entertainment or as employment (such as giving toastmaster speeches, making announcements at club meetings, or being a newspaper reporter).

Total   — — —

---

son's immediate future, near future, and eventual future. Managers with extremely high or low optimism scores on a particular case would be asked to explain where they got specific conclusions.

In this way, managers were held accountable to their peers for demonstrating the evidence on which they based their judgments. This was done repeatedly, for a total of eight cases during the training. This meant that each manager made 240 judgments.

Trends in these judgments were analyzed by a computer, which then wrote each manager a letter explaining the trends and what they might mean. One manager, for example, was told:

Dear Mr. Jameson,
You predicted behavior in these cases about as most managers did—except when the case was about a person with a Spanish surname. In those cases, you were consistently more pessimistic about the person's chances to succeed than you were about blacks, women, or others. No one is calling you prejudiced, but you were out of line with other managers in this regard.

ESTIMATING POTENTIAL: SAMPLE CASE

Donna Cole, Computer Systems Supervisor

You won't find Donna Cole behind one of those housewife's aprons that has big red letters printed: "I spent four years of college for this?" Donna looked for—and found—an outlet for her frustration and determination. Since coming to work for the company, she has organized an informal committee to advise women who feel unfairly passed over for promotion.

When the company refused to announce that her committee had a post office box number employees can write to, Donna took her case directly to the annual stockholders' meeting. Asking for the floor, she gave a short, tough talk—and won some support (although not a majority).

Mrs. Cole is an independent, self-confident, well-traveled woman who likes people. From graphics clerk, in 1955, she rose to her current position of computer systems supervisor in Boston. Her salary shot from $2,500 in 1955 to $26,000 in 1973, and there has to be a reason for a tenfold salary increase in 18 years!

Her performance level is indicated by her last "yearly report." She was stationed in San Francisco then, working with the company laboratories on a computer project, which unfortunately had to be canceled in January. The wrap-up and goodbyes were finished in February, and then she went back to New England.

She was transferred to a new assignment in the CRX computer system in which she staffed, planned, trained, scheduled, and implemented (supervising a staff of thirteen). That job is famous within the company as "the place to which people are transferred and are never heard from again." One mistake in billing and you have to explain why to the president.

Donna says, with some good humor, "I moved into this assignment with trepidation but found the staff the best group of people I have ever worked with. But what a job! Every day was World War II. And that was my major problem—how to change the system so that it was not always a crisis to manage."

Donna developed a new plan and sold it to her boss and higher management. This plan accomplished the following: One key project that had dragged on for four years without being finished was completed. There were far fewer crises: overtime requirements for her staff were reduced by 40 percent during the first six months after implementation of the new plan. The company began assigning new computer supervisors to work with Donna for three months to get broken in before going elsewhere.

Donna Cole was annoyed that replacements sent to her department were rarely women, and she noticed that the new computer supervisors were all men. Feeling she was merely a "token woman," she organized the informal company committee, mentioned before, to help women. She has also helped women in other companies to start a new national association called "Association of Women Entrepreneurs." AWE will try to get more women to own businesses and pressure the government to grant women their fair share of loans.

In college, Donna was a speech major and a top debater. She is attractive, blond, blue-eyed, and 5'6", but has never modeled. She would rather be respected for what she can do than for how she looks.

Another manager was told she was consistently more optimistic about every case involving minority employees. Since the rules on "reverse discrimination" have not been clarified, we made no comment on this pattern—except that the consequences might be to get minority employees promoted beyond their ability to deliver results.

This peer feedback project did not reveal any evidence of "generalized" prejudice. A manager might be consistently pessimistic or optimistic about the chances of blacks, for example, but this had nothing to do with his or her views on women, oriental-Americans, or Spanish-surnamed persons. (Notice that this particular application of measuring objective judgment defines "prejudice" as a deviant use of evidence rather than as an attitude unfavorable to a particular group.)

Objectivity Versus Prejudice

The question might be raised as to whether we should train managers to be open-minded (unprejudiced) toward all groups, and if so, how we should do it. This approach to managers' attitudes has been characteristic of society's approach to prejudice up to this point. This might be called a combined "education and law" approach, which holds that if managers do not change their attitudes but instead make decisions discriminating against certain groups, people will use the law and sue them.

Whatever the merits of the "education and law" approach, this chapter has presented a different view—one that might be called the "training and productivity" approach. It holds that managers should be trained to be objective, not to avoid legal damages, but because predicting performance accurately (and basing employment and promotion decisions on accurate prediction) helps productivity. In short—managers should be objective because objectivity is good business.

9

General Competence: Objective Analysis

Instead of letting impressionistic judgments decide a person's right to a job or promotion, there would seem to be ethical and legal arguments in favor of objective judgments. If objective judgments, moreover, turn out to be more valid, then there would, as noted earlier, be a third argument in favor of the approach presented in the present chapter—greater business value. While the issue has not been finally settled, the findings of most research projects comparing impressionistic judgments with those based on objective procedures have favored the latter.

But what is to be analyzed in the track record? We have used two broad approaches in our work. The first, which will be outlined here, involves analyzing the candidate's track record for evidence of the general competences found necessary for most jobs of a given type—say, nonroutine jobs. The second approach, which will be discussed in the following chapter, requires developing a separate "job model" for each position to be filled and analyzing each candidate's track record for evidence that he or she can effectively produce the results required in that particular job.

General Competences

Before discussing the types of general competences that should be considered as part of a valid selection method, we need to define the criteria a "competence" must meet in order for it to be objectively analyzed and utilized as a basis for selection. These criteria are:

1. A competence must be an observable form of action.
2. The action must generate consequences having economic value to the organization.

Everyone has a list of skills, knowledges, types of motivation, and competences required for "success." We will keep ours short but will hold open the possibility that the list can be expanded at a later point. We regard the following broad competences as basic to effectively getting results on any nonroutine job (a routine job is one demanding repetitive activity, with almost no employee discretion or judgment required; a nonroutine job is one in which the employee makes choices rather than blindly applying policy and following procedure):

Communications. Isn't it almost impossible to imagine a job in a corporation or other organization that does not demand communications competences? We will show how track record and other data can be used to objectively analyze three kinds of communications: spoken, written, and numerical. (Numerical communications is a bit unorthodox, so we will define that below.)

Interpersonal Effectiveness. By almost universal agreement, one must be able to work with people who are higher, lower, or equal in rank in the chain of command. However, there is a problem here as to what is meant by "effectiveness," which makes this kind of evaluation less objective than is the case with communications.

Managerial Effectiveness. Managerial competence refers to the candidate's history of results—and how they were obtained. It is impossible to say that the how does not matter. There are ethical, legal, and other constraints on what is a legitimate way to obtain results—constraints which vary by corporation and by culture. Hence your "scoring system" must vary accordingly.

We will, at this point, pause to repeat an important practical consideration: It is possible—*and desirable*—to combine TRI with *other assessment methods.* There are advantages to every form of assessment. The interview humanizes the employment and promotion process. The test (if it is a test of ability) objectifies the process. Application blanks bring in the candidate's history and track record, although on a very limited basis. Assessment centers afford the opportunity to directly observe the candidate performing simulations of the work.

For these reasons, in the following explanations of how to analyze the above competences, we will freely borrow from these other assessment methods, combining them with the track record data where possible.

Evaluating Communications Competences

It is simple enough to obtain samples of a person communicating in writing or in conversation. Speaking situations (one-on-one, one to a small group, or one to an audience) can be set up in an assessment center and the candidate's performance recorded and scored for effectiveness. It is difficult to even imagine assessment without spoken communications! In fact, the strongest argument in favor of the traditional interview is that it serves as a way of obtaining a sample of the candidate's communications competences.

Writing is somewhat less widely understood as a requirement for managerial and supervisory effectiveness. But it is clear that when management has to communicate with persons who are too numerous to reach through conversation or speech, or who are more than one level removed in the chain of command, the skilled writer becomes indispensable. Moreover, writing plays a vital role in shaping managers' thoughts. As managers write, they can glance back and critique their own planning or analysis. This is not feasible—and is sometimes impossible—while merely "talking things out" with someone. Writing is visible thought.

Numerical communications refers to the ability to use numbers persuasively and realistically. Although no one can deny that all business planning has an indispensable basis in figures, it does not seem to me that the most common need in business is for people with advanced mathematical preparation. This is not, however, because of the advent of computing (and hand calculators), because no conceivable software program is going to relieve managers of the need to think effectively.

Instead of sheer mathematical ability, what is needed in business is the ability to think quantitatively in terms that will influence others. Numerical communications is a form of leadership—not a chore that can be assigned to the computer or pocket calculator.

To appraise a person's numerical communications competence, you should set up a numerical simulation problem and have the candidate not only solve the problem but convince others that the solution is correct and leads to a desirable business outcome.

Expert Analysis

Before deciding on the ways in which the candidate can provide samples of the above three forms of communications, it is important to distinguish between the following options for how the data will later be analyzed:

- By assessors—persons from the company trained to analyze track record or other data. (This option is not recommended for communications.)
- By experts in each of the three areas of communications. (This option is recommended.)

The reason for recommending analysis by communications experts lies in the immense advantage they offer: Not only can they rate competence (as can trained assessors who are not experts), but they can understand *why* the person cannot communicate well. This permits experts to make recommendations about what the candidate can do to correct the weaknesses.

To analyze spoken communications, I would use speech experts. This implies—in the case of one-on-one communications or one to a small group—the use of a speech therapist or someone with graduate training in speech pathology. In the case of communications with audiences, public speaking instructors with graduate speech training would be required.

As to evaluating written communications, suitable experts can almost always be found among university instructors who combine a liberal arts English education with some appreciation of the modifications customary in business writing.

Regarding numerical communications, I have not yet found the ideal qualifications for an expert. Certainly some knowledge of elementary mathematics and its applications in such areas as profit and loss analysis, cost accounting, and statistical inference is relevant; yet it would be a mistake to confuse this competence with a detailed knowledge of those areas.

Evaluating Interpersonal Competences

The argument for regarding interpersonal competences as a requirement for success is as strong as the argument for communications—but the difficulties of objective appraisal are much greater.

Many believe that an assessment center approach—involving simulations or role playing of interpersonal situations—permits assessors to observe what a candidate is "really" like in working with people. However, it is doubtful that such an approach provides a representative sample of what the candidate has done or ordinarily does. Others believe in personality questionnaires. But, at best, these provide opinions about interpersonal relationships rather than descriptions.

Instead, interpersonal relations should be appraised by systematically questioning the candidate about his or her track record and then analyzing that record for the kinds of interpersonal relationships shown in it. To the extent that the TR contains verifiable events, this approach will yield more solid information. As a cross-check on the information, you can:

- Question peers and the immediate superior if the candidate is an employee.
- Simulate interpersonal relations situations, as in an assessment center, to see if the findings agree with the TR data.

We need to know the candidate's typical behavior in at least the following situations:

1. Working with immediate superiors.
2. Working with peers.
3. Working with subordinates.

A still more comprehensive assessment would include the candidate's relations with others one-on-one, one to several, and one to many persons at once. "One-on-one relations" has an obvious meaning; "one to several" refers to small-group situations. What about "one to many"? This refers to situations in which the other actors are not all in the same room. For example, a sales manager may have friction with the entire sales force in the eastern United States.

What we would like to know is how effective the candidate has been. But in practice, "effectiveness" is a relative term. What is considered effective in one company is perceived as wishy-washy in another. Therefore it is probably more important to see whether the candidate's approach to interpersonal relations matches the style of the hiring company (its "culture") or that of the persons with whom the candidate will be working.

Expert Analysis
In contrast to the recommendation made for analyzing communications competences, interpersonal relations should be evaluated by trained coders who understand the culture in which the job exists. This is not because there are no experts in interpersonal relations, but rather because such judgments can be made by coders, and the use of experts should be reserved for unusual and complex cases.

Evaluating Managerial Competences

For many, managerial competences are the only dimension. While this is erroneous, I would accept it as essential to know the candidate's managerial competences, even if communications and interpersonal relations are unknown.

A manager's effectiveness consists of such competences (in order of increasing importance) as setting goals, persisting in spite of obstacles, and obtaining results despite those obstacles. Some would see goal setting as more significant than persisting. But few would dispute that the most essential information in a TR is the candidate's past results.

Goal Setting. In assessing the candidate's ability with respect to goal setting, it is necessary to examine the TR account for evidence that he or she looked ahead, examined alternatives, and set priorities in past jobs. Coders can be trained to make this determination. However, many client corporations like to review the written yearly summaries prepared by managers undergoing TR assessment. The most useful single report for this purpose is perhaps the simplest of all: It is shown in Figure 13.

Obstacles. One of the great advantages of the TR approach is the view it affords of the person's past working environments. The candidate's yearly reports should be examined for what they show of the outside factors he or she has contended with in the past. In many ways, behavior in the face of obstacles reveals more of a manager's competences than behavior in situations permitting leisurely goal setting.

However, here is a fine point: The word "competence" sounds as if we are interested only in what the manager does, but in fact, we are very much interested in the challenges and hardships the manager has faced and endured. In many ways, these reveal more of the toughness of effective managers than do their skills.

There is a second reason for interest in outside obstacles: It is far easier for a candidate to discuss obstacles than to discuss failures. Typically a person will say: "That year we faced a major threat from new foreign competition—and higher production costs in our South Chicago plant." Such a candidate is talking about the external environment rather than about his or her approach to getting the job done. But there is no realistic way to understand managerial action without perceiving it in the context of such environmental conditions. Then the manager may go on to discuss the negative impact of those external conditions on profits and the other goals not met that year. This is a customary way of speaking or reporting and is not at all a sign that the manager is concealing failure or distorting the TR.

Results. By "results," we mean economically significant outcomes rather than just whether a manager met all his or her goals. This is not to say that a high record of achievement in the manager's personal goals is unimportant. But the TR system calls for

Figure 13. Summary of operating results: 19xx.

During this year, you were accountable for the organization's or your own investment. An investment was made in you by the organization. You invested *your* time and effort. What have you or others to show for it? Consider what you started and tried to do and either succeeded at, failed at, or left unfinished. What was the tangible result from each such effort?

Outline this yearly report below, listing the end results and shortfalls as if you were going to make a report to your superiors.

_____

_____

_____

_____

_____

_____

_____

_____

_____

_____

_____

_____

_____

_____

_____

_____

_____

_____

_____

learning how what the manager did fits into the organization and produced a payoff there. In general, such significant organizational results fall into five classes:

- Profits, cost control, or sales.
- Production quantity or quality.
- Producing an innovation of economic significance.
- Eliminating bureaucratic interference with any of the above results.
- Maintaining organizational cohesion, including adherence to policy.

These five classes of results are listed in decreasing order or importance. (Of course, that reflects my own values and experience, and readers may differ violently.)

The candidate's TR should be studied for the frequency, type, and significance of the above results in it. There are wide individual differences. Some managers report almost no results, despite suggestions that this is what they are paid for. Others emphasize the results they have been producing at the expense of credibility. That is, if a manager lists many impressive results without any corresponding account of how they were obtained, there is no way to be sure they were produced by that manager.

A Sample Track Record

Richard S. was the top prospect among 12 managers appraised for the New England Corporation. This determination was based on a detailed analysis of his track record. In the assessment procedure followed, the candidates each prepared a biography of the last decade and three yearly reports.

What follows is Richard's biography (for the sake of brevity, it has been condensed and is shown here in the third person—written about Richard rather than by him), the three yearly reports as he prepared them, and a discussion of how Richard's track record was assessed to determine his competences.

SAMPLE TR: RICHARD S.

Biography

Bright, serious, and ambitious, Richard S. is a self-confident man. After graduating with honors from college, he rose from supervisory assistant in W. in 1965 to his present job as district plant manager in Q. During this time, his salary jumped from $6,600 to $25,840.

Passed over for a promotion and transferred to Rhode Island in 1967, Mr. S. overcame discouragement and adjusted to the new atmosphere. Showing his communications talents, he achieved lasting accomplishments in public relations despite boredom with his 1968 job. The result? A promotion.

At the district level in 1971, he continued upward, leading the New England Corporation in production and cost control in 1972 and receiving the honor of an "outstanding" appraisal rating.

Forceful enough to make necessary management replacements in order to keep pace with company goals, in 1973 Mr. S. developed subordinates and achieved his objectives.

With another promotion disappointment in 1974, Mr. S. again overcame depression and rebuilt his shaken confidence while coping with tensions on the job. He led the division in results during the first quarter and also developed subordinates for promotion.

Definite in his goals, Mr. S.'s concern is how to change his own life rather than how to change external factors. Happy with his family, he likes the challenge, responsibility, and status of his job but dislikes both his supervisor and the long working hours. He is anxious for a change of assignment.

Feeling politically inept and perhaps too outspoken and trusting, Mr. S. sometimes wonders how much hard work will achieve for him, and his home life comes to seem more important than his work. More often, Richard S. is extremely confident about his own resources, he is hard-working, results-oriented, and ambitious in business and life, and he feels that the future looks promising.

Annual Report: 1972

My first year as district plant manager was 1972. Not knowing what to expect, we had set "stretch" goals for that year. The response from my team was excellent. In summary, the district led the company in production and attendance, was second in service and sales, and was third in set control for the year.

Our weak spot was safety: Careless, preventable motor vehicle accidents continued to plague us. To reduce this problem, we developed an extensive safety operational review that was later used for the rest of the division. We began to see the fruits of our efforts by the last quarter.

I was appraised an "O" (outstanding) in 1972, and since that was my first field assignment in the plant department, I was extremely pleased. It was decided that I was ready for a larger and more complex district, so I was reassigned to the Q. district at the end of the year.

Annual Report: 1973

I was transferred to the Q. district in November 1972, so 1973 was my first full year on the job. We had some early successes: Production improved because of controls that were put into place. I replaced management personnel who could not keep pace with corporate goals. This was difficult in some cases, while in other cases the foremen were happy to be taken off the firing line.

By the end of the first quarter, things really started to move. The report rate, an indicator of our speed in answering a customer's complaints, had been reduced from 7.5 to 5.8, and production had gone from last in the division to second in the division. Union relations were solidified.

In May, we cut over the New State Bank Complex without a hitch. The vice-president called to congratulate our team. We had an operational review in Q. by the general office staff and were given a clean bill of health.

The rain and lightning storms that came in July 1973 caused a momentary setback to our plans because of the extensive damage, but we recovered and by the end of the year had established ourselves as a competitive district.

Annual Report: 1974

My district shot out of the gate toward achieving its objectives in 1974. By the end of the first quarter, we had led our division in results for three months in a row. By the end of the second quarter, we had led the division five out of the first six months.

Production had improved approximately 34 percent. Service as measured by reports per 100 stations had improved 22 percent—second best in the New England Corporation.

To date in 1974, we have promoted three craftsmen to first-line supervisors, and three of my first-line supervisors have been promoted to managers within our division.

Aside from weak spots that popped up on installation service in June and an absence problem in March, which was corrected, 1974 appears to be running the way we had planned.

Discussion. Richard S. reported accomplishing many business objectives. The natural question arises as to how we can know whether this is true. In a promotion situation such as this, the verification process calls for obtaining independent data from Richard's immediate superiors during the three years covered by his yearly reports.

It would have been too easy for Richard's superiors to confirm his yearly reports if they favored his candidacy. For that reason, we did not show them his account of each year but asked what, specifically, they had observed to be his accomplishments or short-falls that year. The facts Richard reported were confirmed.

In a larger project, in which 55 managers were appraised for promotion, we had another occasion to conduct such independent confirmations of the facts given in their yearly reports. Following the same procedure—in which we did not share the report with their bosses (sometimes, three bosses for one candidate during the preceding three years)—we confirmed 90 percent of the facts. This finding is typical of the reliability of the method.

The only reason we obtained such reliability, however, was probably our having limited the verification to *facts*. That is, we did not ask the candidates' immediate superiors to evaluate them. In my opinion, the reliability of the TR system is high for the facts it delivers, but the reliability of opinions in performance review is notoriously low. Hence, there is no reason to lose the advantage of TR by mixing it up with such performance ratings.

In the example of Richard S., the track record results are given in qualitative form. It is possible, however, to quantify his competences in terms of percentile scores—by comparing him with other candidates who have previously been evaluated in this manner. These percentile scores were in fact computed in his case. His overall suitability for a general management position was at the eightieth percentile, which is very high. Richard's results-oriented score (we called it the "performance index" at that time) was 63 percent, which is also higher than that of most managers who have been appraised.

Richard's general management score was based on all three of the areas assessed—communications (spoken, written, and quantitative), interpersonal relations, and managerial effectiveness. The reason his general management score was higher than his results-oriented score was peculiar to that industry (in which all managers, because of the way the corporations were organized, to have a lower tendency to report results than were likely managers in other industries).

10

Chances to Succeed in a Particular Job: Objective Analysis

The track record and related data can be objectively analyzed against the broad competences required to perform certain types of management jobs in general or against the specific competences required to perform one particular job. The foregoing chapter outlined the general approach; this chapter will describe the specific approach. To apply the system presented in this chapter, you will need a job model (discussed in Chapter 3). Using this system, the question for assessment becomes:

How close a match do we have—between this job model and this particular candidate's TR?

Answering such a question is in many ways harder than answering the questions about general competences in the preceding chapter. But if you can make an accurate forecast for performance in a particular job, you will gain the advantages of rifle fire rather than shotgun blasts. (There are situations demanding either weapon, of course.)

Suppose you have to choose among three candidates for a transfer to Brussels. The issue may narrow down to a question such as this:

Which candidate speaks fluent French and can persuade our Brussels supplier to adopt and maintain our new quality production standards in manufacturing the new heat regulator?

Such a question cannot logically be translated into the scheme used in the previous chapter. Assuming that all three candidates speak fluent French, there is no further value in knowing which one gets the highest communications score. Knowledge about the candidate's interpersonal relations competence in general would also be too broad to permit a determination of whether the candidate could meet the above specific requirement. That is, it would be possible for a manager to be very effective in dealing with most people—but not with the particular supplier in Brussels.

In a case such as this, we still need a detailed TR, but we will analyze it in a very different way. The following sections will discuss two basic approaches for using the track record to assess a candidate's stability for a particular job. The first is to evaluate the candidate's track record to determine if he or she has demonstrated the ability to produce the *results* specified in the job model. The second is to evaluate the candidate's track record to determine if he or she has demonstrated the *action qualities* considered essential for performing the job.

Assessing the Candidate's Ability to Produce Results

To show how the job model can be used to assess a candidate's ability to produce results, we will review the example of a personnel manager's position, for which the job model specified that the successful candidate must be able to work with the relocation of personnel when various operations were closed down and, in so doing, produce the following outcomes:

A. Developing operating policies, procedures, and performance standards regarding the placement and transfer of personnel.
B. Bypassing bureaucratic roadblocks paralyzing the organization.
C. Developing subordinates in the department.
D. Pursuing these actions even if working for a boss who has "abdicated."

E. Overcoming the resistance of managers who might not want to have personnel relocated into their operations.
F. Coordinating effectively with manpower planning councils and local government officials.
G. Analyzing the competences and transferability of older workers who are especially vulnerable to cutbacks in the corporate payroll.

A two-stage procedure was followed. The candidates for the position were first trained to prepare critical (key) incidents from their own track records that would demonstrate their ability to produce results A through G listed above. (These critical incidents were recorded on the track record form, a sample of which is shown in Figure 14. To condense the sample form for presentation here, the number of blank lines on it has been reduced considerably.) The critical incidents were then evaluated for evidence of probable success in the job.

On the following pages are examples of the critical incidents prepared by Henry Johnston, one candidate for the personnel manager's position. Although all names, places, and titles in the critical incidents have been changed to protect the identities of those involved (the incidents are actually from a different region of the United States than that indicated), the candidate's writing style has purposely been retained.

CRITICAL INCIDENTS

Candidate's Name: Henry Johnston

A. In 1964, I was selected by the director for assignment to Washington to develop new training units in interviewing for the use of federal and state agencies. Working with federal training supervisors and several from the states (of Arizona, Michigan, South Carolina, and Utah), we completed, published, and distributed the training units. All the state agencies used them for a number of years to retain interviewers on the fundamental steps and procedures in hiring. (Note: This candidate then took an industrial job.)

(text continued page 130)

Figure 14. Track record.

Candidate's Name:_____

Please indicate below the evidence (the critical incident) from your track record that indicates you can produce each result. You may add a page of evidence regarding any result if you wish. If you do so, be sure to indicate the letter of the result to which it applies.

A. The following evidence (from the track record) indicates that I can produce result A:

_____

_____

_____

B. The following evidence (from the track record) indicates that I can produce result B:

_____

_____

_____

C. The following evidence (from the track record) indicates that I can produce result C:

_____

_____

_____

D. The following evidence (from the track record) indicates that I can produce result D:

_____

_____

_____

E. The following evidence (from the track record) indicates that I can produce result E:

_____

_____

_____

F. The following evidence (from the track record) indicates that I can produce result F:

_____

_____

_____

G. The following evidence (from the track record) indicates that I can produce result G:

_____

_____

_____

Our evaluation of the track record against the job model for the position of:

_____

Results Likely If Hired:	Action Qualities Shown:
Strong _____	Strong _____
Moderate _____	Moderate _____
Not Shown _____	Not Shown _____

Signature of Evaluator: _____

B. In January 1973, on my return to the company as western Massachusetts district manager, I found the Springfield office and its satellites with ineffective, apathetic top management staff; poor morale; poor community image; demoralized, disorganized, and insufficient—yet qualified—staff working in poor facilities; insufficient and heavy workloads that resulted in poor performance. Working with management and staff, I started a major reorganization and improvement program, and at the end of 1973, I wrote an evaluation of the reasons for past poor performance and of the improvements that had been made and were recommended. Despite improvement in morale and spirit because of my initiative, leadership, and example, since my transfer, the facilities, working conditions, and understaffing, as well as other problems, have not been eliminated because of inadequate resources.

C. In 1974, on my return to Boston as regional director, armed with more responsibility and independent authority on a decentralized basis, I undertook a major reorganization of the regional staff. My intention was to develop a team with more expertise and wider responsibilities—a team of generalists (line-staff combinations)—in the face of limited resources. Hoping to get more results with fewer staff, I reassigned two personnel specialists to local operations in Bedford where they were urgently needed to bolster the training services, consolidated the job information and classification services under one supervisor for the region, and transferred several other functions to my associate. This made a compact team with fewer but more versatile staff.

D. In the 1956–66 period, as Boston manager, I worked under a boss who, although considerate and gentle, was totally ineffective in carrying out his duties because of his many personal problems. They were so severe that he was eventually forced into retirement. The managers in his district operated largely without his guidance and direction. As manager in the largest office where my boss was headquartered, I had a continuous insight into his poor performance but helped him carry out neglected assignments and avoid missed deadlines, as did other managers. His superiors knew about his problems for years but never tried to help him overcome them.

E. In 1974, in answer to long-standing complaints from the apparel and shoe divisions about their inability to find enough stitchers and qualified, tested clerical workers (typists and stenographers) to fill their urgent needs, I inaugurated—in cooperation with the director of the David Hale Training Trade School, the director of the Worcester County Employers Association, and the president of the Office Managers Association—a series of 15 stitching courses and 4 clerical retraining courses for persons we needed to move out of obsolete occupations. This program received national attention through the Department of Labor.

F. In February 1975, I helped set up the Springfield area manpower council. I attended and contributed to all meetings, served as chairman of the review committee, and provided the manpower staff with needed labor market research. I worked with Mayor Suliman, Chairman Walter Kane, and others on the committee and was given a citation in March 1976 for these services by Mayor Suliman.

G. In 1966, I supervised the Worcester older worker study—part of the classic seven cities study conducted nationally by the U.S. Department of Labor. I planned, organized, and implemented all community activities—including obtaining endorsements from 20 agencies and groups; wrote many articles and feature stories for the local news media—including foreign language media, industrial organs, weekly and daily newspapers, radio programs, and information leaflets to applicants; gave talks; and participated in forums and panels during and after the study. In addition to enlisting community participation, interest, and support, I supervised a ten-month study that involved researching the employment and employability problems of 200 control and 200 experimental "over-45" employees in a scientific sampling of specific characteristics and problems. The study required a staff of 20 interviewers and specialists. Upon completion of the study, I assisted the Department of Labor in writing its conclusions.

Note the abundant detail in these critical incidents. Each candidate had been carefully instructed that the credibility of his or her TR depended on whether the incidents could be verified. Verification, in turn, was possible only if names and dates were given. (Names are altered or deleted in the above example, however.) Note, also, that these incidents reveal the candidate's ways of analyzing situations as well as of reporting them.

Each critical incident was reviewed by a panel of three officials who had been trained in the assessment method—especially in the standards of credibility. If a key incident seemed to the panel to be vague, for example, the policy was not to credit the incident with any relevance to the job model at all. Certain data could also be rejected as overblown and unconvincing if the panel decided that an individual was merely engaging in a bit of bureaucratic self-puffery.

But if the critical incident was considered credible, the panel's next task was to decide whether it supported optimism that the candidate would actually be able to effectively produce the specified result. For example, the first critical incident in the example above described an event in 1964—an event which was regarded by the panel as highly credible. But the candidate was given little credit for it, because the incident only told what the candidate did and not how effectively he performed. On the other hand, the panel thought well of the actions reported in the 1973 event, considering them to be good evidence that the candidate would be able to produce result B—overcoming bureaucratic roadblocks.

The reliability of such matching judgments varies with how precisely defined are the results in the job model the panel is working with. In general, the finding in that project was that the three panelists agreed that an incident did (or did not) support a candidate's competence to produce a particular result in from 75 percent to 85 percent of the incidents.

In evaluating each critical incident, it is important that the panel consider all the results to which that incident might apply. That is, an incident that the candidate submits as evidence supporting result A may, in fact, be even stronger evidence for another result as well. The scoring sheet used by one panel (in a hypothetical case) is shown in Table 1.

The tallies show the number of panelists who considered each particular incident to be evidence of competence in regard to the result indicated. You can also see the instances in which panelists regarded a particular incident as evidence of competence in several

Table 1. Critical incidents scoring sheet.

Result	A	B	C	D	E	F	G	Total
A	//	/		/	//			6
B		///	///	//				8
C			///		///	/	///	10

areas—sometimes other than the area that the incident was intended to support. A higher total for a result indicates that the panel felt there was greater evidence supporting the candidate's previous experience (or track record) in that area. In the practical assessment situation, it would be wise to ignore tallies in which only one panelist saw evidence supporting a particular result. This would reduce the scores in Table 1 somewhat.

The last portion of the track record form (Figure 14, shown earlier) has a summary section headed "Results Likely If Hired." This section would be used to record the results of the above kind of analysis. For example, if the panel considered the evidence too weak to support result A, "A" would be written under "Not Shown." If result B were considered moderately well supported, "B" would be written after "Moderate." Finally, if result C were considered well supported, "C" would be written after "Strong."

You will notice that the Track Record form also has a second summary section for recording analysis results, headed "Action Qualities Shown." This summary permits the track record data to be scored for its relevance to the job model in another way, which will be discussed in the following section.

Assessing the Candidate's Action Qualities

A job model may .demand a certain type of person. It may be apparent that a very aggressive individual, with no hesitation about reversing the precedents accepted in a particular office, will be needed to bring about results.

Instead of focusing on the results, as above, the panel evaluating the candidate's track record may prefer to focus on the characteristic actions that they think are essential to success in that particular job. To some extent, these required "action qualities" are reflected in the goal or results statement for the job. However, they represent *how* the effective candidate is expected to operate rather than the end products of that operation.

Based on my experience appraising a large number of managerial candidates, I can offer the following list of 17 action qualities (AQs) that are often considered the modus operandi of the effective model manager. Also indicated is the most appropriate method for assessing each action quality. The AQs are arranged in rough order of the time-span over which they are demonstrated. For example, "Providing long-term, persuasive generalist leadership" cannot be seen in a brief critical incident.

In any particular job model, only four or five of these action qualities might be featured. (If you try to find all 17 in any one candidate, you will be demanding the impossible.) It is practical to settle on the four or five AQs most needed and analyze the candidate's track record for their presence or absence.

ACTION QUALITIES

Demonstrated in Effective Critical Incidents of Managerial Work

1. Providing long-term, persuasive generalist leadership.
   This AQ involves both the ability to foresee possible future events and the sustained drive to get the organization to move toward those events that are desirable. We discovered this action quality to be present in the biographies of eminent leaders but not in those of leaders of good but only local reputation.
   • Assess only through the track record.

2. Providing a major influence on economic survival.
   This AQ refers to obtaining and making money. Like the first AQ above, it requires generalist leadership, but exercised specifically within the economic area. This AQ consists of the many strategies and actions orchestrated toward economic output. It is derived from organization theory, although we developed empirical measures of it in work with several corporations.
   • Assess only through the track record.

3. Inducing sluggish bureaucracy to act.
   This AQ refers to intervention in a situation in which the maintenance of existing policy is self-defeating for the organization. We have observed this AQ in managers' histories, wherein it is likely to flare up abruptly and even dramatically. It is usually followed by a bad performance rating. We also have observed it in high-level selling.

- Assess only through the track record. Must be carefully distinguished from mere trouble-making and boat-rocking.

4. Confronting difficult situations.

This AQ refers to the tendency to search out situations of progressively greater difficulty. In sales, the person will go after very inaccessible or highly resistive accounts. In most careers, there are hurdles whose height provides an incentive to the person with this AQ.

- Assess only through the track record.

5. Inducing growth and innovation.

Unlike the third AQ, this AQ refers to the objective result or output of growth or innovation. A manager who demonstrates this AQ is consistently cited by subordinates as contributing to their growth, and they tend to get promoted. Or the manager produces patents or generates new products, or is observed to "strike sparks" in operating meetings or training sessions. In a typical project involving research and development administrators who demonstrated this AQ, the administrators were shown to induce growth by the way they mediated conflicts among research personnel.

- Assess only through the track record. There are some measures of creativity available, but we are not yet convinced they predict this action quality.

6. Providing quality products or services.

This is the "get-it-done" quality in management, with particular reference to producing a tangible result having salability. It is easiest to perceive this action quality at work in manufacturing, but it is by no means limited to that line of work. In medicine, it would involve producing health services that meet high quality standards.

- Assess only through the track record.

7. Maintaining cohesion and order.

This AQ involves bringing together people, resources, and processes. It has to do with maintaining the organization, its policies, and its procedures. It is "business as usual," and—if not overworked—it is the AQ that makes an organization an organization. It is more the business of staff than of line managers, but there are some production operations requiring this AQ for successful management. Probably all bureaucratic and routine organizations stress it.

  • Assess only through the track record.

8. Maintaining tenacity in pursuit of goals.
This AQ is essentially that of persistence. It is at times "antisocial" in that the manager demonstrating this AQ must ignore feedback that some people give—that his or her idea is useless, that "it is never done that way," or that it isn't worth it. The manager has to learn to ignore some customers' objections and resistance. Such a manager appears a bit dense, seemingly ignoring what others are saying that does not agree with his or her "inner drumbeat." However, this appearance is deceiving, as a truly tenacious manager is not indifferent to all feedback but rather is selective about when and where he or she will accept it. Such a manager *will* respond to outstanding superiors, peers, subordinates, or customers. The projects in which we observed this AQ to be critical included a survey of eminent managers and a study of pharmaceuticals sales.

  • Assess only through the track record.

9. Applying quantitative analysis.
This AQ refers to having "a good head for figures" if one is in general management. In fields such as engineering, the requirements go further. There is a quantitative element in almost any line of work in management. However, the emphasis on application means that the use of these tools is subordinated to the purposes of the work at hand.

  • Difficult to assess through the track record. Easier to assess through academic examination; however, it must be remembered that this is a quality of *action,* not of knowledge.

10. Judging potential.
In making a wide range of decisions, managers must estimate the potential for performance of individuals. These may be subordinates, superiors, or peers. Even in marketing, managers must estimate the potential interest of a customer. This AQ calls for analyzing evidence and forecasting verifiable events. We have completed a very large number of surveys in which we measured good judgment in managers and used training to help improve this AQ.

137

- Difficult to assess through the track record. Laboratory methods of measuring and training managers in this AQ are available.

11. Judging performance.

This AQ is related to the tenth AQ. However, instead of forecasting results based on evidence, judging performance starts with a known result and reconstructs its *causes*. This is probably the critical skill underlying management that gets work out.

- Can be assessed both on the job and in the laboratory. Some managers, for example, never appraise the performance of employees at all; some appraise it badly; and an apparently select few are masters at this particular AQ.

12. Managing under pressure.

This AQ is shown by the manager who stays cool under pressure and does not allow it to disrupt the organization.

- Can best be assessed by having the manager do it himself or herself—by keeping a "working log" and recording the stresses observed over a period of time.

13. Knowing people—perceiving them as individuals.

This AQ is shown by the manager who takes the trouble to note, recall, and use data about individuals on the job. He or she is then ready to make decisions that are supported by evidence. Sales representatives also make good use of this quality as they build up a body of knowledge about customers.

- Assess both through the track record and through laboratory procedures.

14. Fact finding.

This AQ implies both the ability to "get the story" from people and the inclination to want to get to the bottom of what is going on. It has many applications, from interviewing candidates for jobs to investigating accidents and grievances.

- Not difficult to measure through both the track record and laboratory methods.

15. Using flexibility in influence styles.

This AQ refers to choosing which of the available leadership and influence styles best fits a given situation—and then using that style to exercise power. Flexibility (or "contingency management") is paramount. In my research on eminent managers, I found flexibility increased as the managers' level increased; the less eminent were limited to fairly hard-nosed styles whatever the situation.

- Best assessed through analysis of the track record, because the history of a manager is largely the history of the exercise of power. However, laboratory exercises and questionnaires are also available.

16. Reporting to someone.

This AQ involves the ability to be accountable to someone. It has been our observation that learning to work for someone is a neglected area of education and training. There is, however, a keen interest among managers in learning to cope with this AQ.

- Both the track record and laboratory methods are appropriate for assessment of this AQ.

17. Knowledge of a specialized field.

This AQ refers to the application of a manager's knowledge rather than only the possession of it.

- May be appraised from a transcript or résumé but is more precisely assessed through the track record.

A typical scoring sheet used by one panel (in a hypothetical case) to record the critical incidents from the track record that illustrate that the candidate demonstrates the required AQs is shown in shortened form in Table 2.

Table 2 displays the form for recording the evaluations of seven critical incidents for evidence of three action qualities (11, 13, and 14). AQs 12 and 15 were not required by the hypothetical job, a low-pressure job that did not call for flexibility. A similar form might be used to appraise an action quality such as long-term leadership (AQ 1). However, in that case, annual reports should also be used. (See Figure 13.)

The following paragraphs compare action qualities with several other personal characteristics that are sometimes assessed during the selection process.

Action Qualities Versus Competences. The term "competency" is currently fashionable. An action quality is much like a competency but includes environmental or situational factors. A second impor-

Table 2. Excerpt, critical incidents scoring sheet: action qualities 11–15.

AQ	In the Job Model?	Incident							Total
		A	B	C	D	E	F	G	
11	Yes			///		///	///		9
12	No								—
13	Yes			//			///	//	7
14	Yes			///	/	//	///		9
15	No								—

tant difference is in the restriction of action qualities to the analysis of track records. That is, there are no "tests" of AQs. AQs are always shown on the job or in some other "real-time" situation. But in general, many of the same arguments that support competency assessment also favor assessment of AQs.

Action Qualities Versus Traits. A "trait" is a personal characteristic. For example, a person may be "extroverted" or "intelligent." An AQ, however, is a characteristic of action and occurs not "within the person" but in an observed situation.

Action Qualities Versus Behaviors. A "behavior," like a "trait," is a psychological characteristic. However, actions are things done in a person's job role that are significant because they obtain (or fail to obtain) an economic result. A sale is obtained through an action of a certain kind—an action quality. But the salesperson may simultaneously be showing many other behaviors that have nothing to do with selling.

Which System of Analysis Is Best?

We have now reviewed three objective systems of analysis. In the preceding pages, we outlined the general competences approach. In this chapter we outlined two ways to match a candidate's track record against a particular job model: by estimating the likelihood that he will obtain each specified result and by estimating to what extent he possesses the key AQs implied by the job model.

The *general competences* approach is the simplest. We do not have to study each job but can simply use the same assessment procedures over and over. This will increase the procedures' precision as we experience the blessings of large statistics—but at the cost of decreased relevance to the particular job.

The *results-oriented* approach is the most complex. It requires that we estimate the likelihood that a candidate will attain certain unique results that we may never have to forecast again. Concentrating on one-time events seems like (and is) a great expense. However, there is a great gain in relevance, and this is absolutely essential if the result sought is critical. For example, suppose we have to forecast whether an astronaut will be able to leave the space capsule in ten seconds, once it has landed on the moon. This event is so critical that an assessment panel would focus on it intensively, even though they had never before made exactly the same forecast (and never will again).

The *action quality* approach is in between: It has the advantages of both the general competences and the results-oriented approaches. There are jobs which specify action but for which the results cannot routinely be measured. Yet we want to be relevant—to select personnel who will produce results-relevant action. An example is "Sales Support" personnel. Although we would use the results-oriented approach to select the *sales representative*, we would use action qualities to select the support team. Like the general competences approach, it enables us to learn to become more reliable and build up statistics on a large number of cases. Action quality statistics are a bit "messier" than those obtained in the general competences approach, because in one case we might assess AQs No. 1 through No. 5, and in another case, AQs No. 2 through No. 6, for example. But we can at least choose the kind of action qualities we want to use for assessment.

11

Reorienting Your Selection Policies

The problem with selection policy is how to reorient it to the goal of productivity—in a measurable way. That is, we need to apply the concept of productivity by revising policies in an operational way, not merely by giving "lip service." By *operational*, I mean that the design for collecting and evaluating candidates' data must be *factually* shown to enhance corporate productivity.

Unfortunately, the concept of "productivity" is also used in a trendy manner. This is common among those who continue to use traditional selection methods as if their connection with productivity had been demonstrated—which is rarely the case.

But how can we demonstrate that the TR method works any better? In earlier chapters, we alluded to research in the method without outlining this evidence in any systematic way. Most of this research supports certain general principles of behavioral consistency, which in turn supports our optimism that track record data will turn out to be predictive when used operationally. However, such optimism has to be *rejustified* in each particular company and in each individual job. Validation is a continuous necessity in the selection of personnel. It is discussed in this chapter as an integral part of the implementation process.

What Is Productivity?

If "productivity" is something that individual behavior achieves, then we can examine how this behavior can be identified and facilitated. Unfortunately, this is not the meaning given to the term by everyone. Some other meanings—*counterproductive* as far as I am concerned—are that productivity is:

- Concerned only with what "workers" do, not with what others (such as managers) do.
- Concerned only with "production" and not with other functions, such as marketing and finance.
- Dramatically improved only by installing labor-saving equipment.
- A slogan that we attach to every practice or policy we want to promote, in order to elicit top management support.

We will now examine these misconceptions about productivity.

Workers Versus Managers. The "worker" is traditionally regarded as the primary producer, while others—the staff and higher management—presumably "watch the work done," in the words of the old labor song. On the contrary: We had better learn to measure the productivity of the many jobs that, on the surface, do not appear to generate products. These include service, office, research, and—quite obviously—supervisory and managerial positions. These jobs are not accurately called "labor" and cannot be well understood through the concepts of "labor economics."

This traditional thinking leads many to attribute the losses in American productivity (or the English or French productivity problems) to the worker—a conclusion that is poorly thought through as well as irritating. From where I stand, there are several industries in the United States in which colossal errors in judgment by management caused collapses in productivity, dwarfing any alleged labor slowdowns or indifference. The worker is included in our considerations about selecting for productivity, but the TR methods probably make their best contributions at higher levels where, assuredly, we had better care about productivity.

Production Versus Productivity. The semantic confusion between "production" and "productivity" continues. The two terms look similar, but why center our productivity goals upon the production department? We should also be asking how "productive" the sales department is. Peter Drucker, from the beginning of his writing, emphasized marketing as the major objective of the corporation.

Equipment Versus People. It is a short step from the overemphasis on production to a preoccupation with equipment and other hardware. This is not a bias fostered by the production department, however. I am inclined to think it a bias created by the human mind itself. Throughout the history of social change, innovation has proceeded fastest when it came in the form of a tangible gadget or object. The astute observation has been made that the ball-point pen spread around the world faster than the idea of democracy.

Today's revolution in information processing began with computer hardware (even though it now evolves through developments in the less-tangible software). Thus, human perception more quickly grasps objects, and we therefore call them "tangible" or "practical." But the real explanation of productivity is not always (and perhaps not even usually) found in equipment. A good example is the Japanese productivity advantage. Is it explained by their different conception of how human effort is to be organized or by their access to technology? Both are true. But if I had to choose one explanation, it would be the Japanese approach to the organization of effort.

The point of the foregoing example is not to propose that we imitate Japanese social organization but to suggest that we recognize that productivity has a great deal to do with the organization of effort. While the truth of this remark seems obvious, unfortunately, the "tangible" aspects of productivity continue to receive our first attention.

Productivity as Provable, Versus Its Use as a Slogan. The emphasis in the TR method is on a person's past output. This output is measured if possible; if this is not possible, it is documented as specifically as is feasible. This documentary approach is in dramatic contrast to the use of "productivity" as a slogan or battle cry. One advertising brochure said, "Use our interviewer-training method for greater productivity." Such slogan-mongering that substitutes for thought is characteristic of green managers when they try to whip up an interest among subordinates in "higher profits."

If the above semantic confusions are avoided, we are ready for serious consideration of how to demonstrate the productive, profitable consequences of using track records. In general, this demonstration results from the "predictive validation" of the system, provided what is predicted are tangible business results. An example to be discussed below is the prediction of sales volume.

Implementing a Track Record System

Implementation of a track record system would involve the following broad phases:

- Selling top management on the system.
- Developing and implementing job models.
  or
- Developing and implementing a competences design.
- Validating.

Selling Top Management
Some, but not all, of the corporate top management may be excited about the possibilities of reorienting the selection process. What can be said to those who are not? You might try to obtain approval for a pilot demonstration in an area of the business where most of the executive group would accept the available measurements of productivity in performance. Then you could use the TR system and compare the productivity levels of the candidates having favorable track records with the other candidates. For many industries, that area of the business would be the sales division. The advantages are obvious: There is almost always a keen interest in improving sales, and measuring productivity performance in that division would be relatively free of the difficulties involved in measuring the productivity of more abstract work.

Developing and Implementing Job Models
Having convinced top management to take at least the initial steps toward implementing a new selection system, you should identify one or more key jobs and build job models. (See Chapter 3.)

If you elect to do this in the sales area, there are, again, conspicuous advantages that will help build interest and support for the program. By comparing the average sales volume produced by those in the sales force who show certain action qualities with the average of those who do not show those AQs, you can measure the potential dollar impact of that job model itself. In other words, if *everyone* did what is shown in the model, it would be worth X dollars.

Just such a project was completed for Digital Equipment Corporation. Leroy Malouf, Fred Zweig, and I collected critical incidents from sales personnel in several countries and used them as the basis for recommending the most economically productive job model possible for what would, in many companies, be called the position of "sales engineer."

The job model provides the "targets" for selection and hence guides the validation effort as well. For example, the TR interviewer attempts to determine whether Jones, the candidate, is likely to attain result A. The validation consists, in essence, in finding out later whether Jones did achieve result A. It should be stressed again that this follow-up determination is *not* the same as finding out what ratings Jones later gets from his or her supervisor. Jones can attain result A without obtaining a good rating from the boss.

Two major steps must be taken to implement the job models. First, you have to train the interviewers in how to collect track record data. Second, you have to train panels or individuals to evaluate those data once they are collected. Then you should use the new procedure long enough to allow the hired or promoted individuals to perform, at which point you can validate the system, as discussed below.

Developing and Implementing a Competences Design
It is not always practical to take time to research the most productive ways of doing each individual job. You have the option, instead, of following the general competences approach, outlined in Chapter 9. You need to decide what competences are necessary for success in all the jobs you are filling or in a certain family of such jobs and then devise a TR method for assessing candidates for these competences.

In the chapter on general competences, it was suggested that you integrate the TR approach with some of the older methods, so that elements of assessment centers and testing are used along with TR to collect and evaluate samples of communications.

Having designed such an integrated system, you can try it out in a pilot program: Train interviewers or others to operate the data-collection system; train individuals or panels to evaluate the competences data; and, finally, give the new procedure a long enough trial period to allow the selected individuals to perform and show how well (or how badly) your new system is working.

Validating

The logic of validation is fundamentally simple, from the TR point of view, if not easy in practice. The logic of TR is historical: *Only if you can predict a valued event is your selection system valid.* This means that "concurrent validation"—such as comparing the TR judgments with those made at the same time using other methods (assessment center ratings, for example)—proves nothing about predictive validity.

You should collect the TRs, evaluate them, lock up the data, and hire or promote the candidates without consulting the data. Later, unlock the files and compare the data with the job outputs. Here again, the only useful data (or "criteria") will be productive data—that is, operating results. You cannot, for example, validate a rigorous track record against a weak criterion. Don't validate the TR against the opinions of the boss or peers, the promotion rates of the candidates, their regularity in attendance, or their turnover. These facts are all important in the operation of a firm, but their connection with productivity is tenuous.

When there is a job model, it guides us in making predictions that the candidate will (or won't) achieve certain results and gives us a certain level of confidence in our predictions. Table 3 is a hypothetical example based on a case in which the selection panel made probability estimates (from zero expectation to 100 percent certainty) that each of the five results would be attained by Jones. These probabilities are ranked from 1 to 5. Jones's actual attainment on the job several months later is also shown. It is expressed not in terms of probability estimates but only in terms of which of the results was most fully attained (ranked 1 among the five),

Table 3. Probability estimates for Jones; forecast versus
actual results.

| | Original TR Forecast | | Actual Results |
Result	Estimate	Rank	Rank
A	90%	2	1
B	100	1	2
C	40	5	4
D	50	4	3
E	60	3	5

which was next most fully attained (ranked 2), and so on down
to 5.

The fit between the predicted and actual results for Jones is
shown by the differences in the ranks. For example, the biggest
"miss" is in regard to result E.

Using another approach, the candidate can be compared with
others doing similar work. Here, the "actual results" column might
consist not of which of the five results was most fully attained, but
of how the candidate compared to the others. These examples, of
course, are not presented as a statistical model; they merely outline
the logic of validation in a highly schematic way.

When there is no job model, we are forecasting competences to
see whether the measure of, say, interpersonal competence obtained during the selection process gave values that accurately
predict how well the candidate later turns out to relate to people on
the job. However, you can also check the competences measures to
see how well they predict later *results* on the job.

Validating the Decision-Makers' Judgments. There is yet another
validation approach that might be a shortcut with great advantages
over the approach discussed above. This is to find out—in spite of
all the doubts that have been raised here about "gut feel"—
whether some of your managers do not indeed turn out to be
superior "menschenkenner" or "people-readers."

The validation method used to research such questions is the
"known case"—that is, cases in which the outcome is known. Such

a case is given to a manager whose people-reading skill is to be measured. The case includes:

1. The data known about the candidate at the original point of hire or promotion.
2. The later performance of that candidate.

The manager reviews No. 1 and forecasts No. 2. You can compare these predictions to see how close a match there is, just as in any validation.

Our findings from such experiments established that some managers were, in fact, very good at this forecasting, while others were not doing much better than pure guessing. Why should these latter managers be entrusted with critical personnel decisions? Let your imagination consider the consequences if we required managers to *prove* they can do an accurate job of selecting personnel! After all, others go out on a limb. Economists publish their forecasts. Sales executives take such public risks repeatedly, whenever they launch a new product or a sales campaign. Why should personnel decision making be risk-free?

Risks of the TR System

Any new system imposes costs—emotional, political, economic, or organizational. The emotional cost of an innovation is in admitting we were wrong, or perhaps too narrow, in our previous position or policies. How many of us resist innovations in hiring or promotion for this reason? The political cost consists of the hazards in managing all change and in settling the conflicts that inevitably arise (as some persons gain advantage and others lose) in any new system. The economic costs are those paid for any new learning, including the training time and the costs of errors until we master the new skills. Finally, the organizational costs consist of all of the above, plus the strain of any change on the organization.

Perhaps such risks hardly need to be mentioned. They are sizable in any major change, and in the end, one has to ask, "Is it worth it?" Until recently, innovation in the field of human resources attracted little attention in some companies. We are using job evaluation systems that are a quarter-century old, and our interviewing techniques may be even older. There has been little innovation in selection since the assessment center.

Perhaps only in training and in organization development has there been innovation of any scope. Yet how widespread is even this innovation? In the greater Boston area, for example, 55 percent of the companies polled provide training for *no one*. As for organization development, professionals in the United States (with influences from West Germany and the United Kingdom) thought that they had invented its techniques. Now, in light of the interest in Japanese social innovations, we must begin to wonder who the innovators really are.

These points are raised not to express doubts about the chances of the TR system or other specific innovations but rather to emphasize the extraordinary opportunity represented by the current intense concern about productivity. The time to seek support for innovation would appear to be *now*.

Size of the Investment Required

How large a part of your costs does the payroll represent? The immense sum may intimidate you to the point where you can scarcely begin thinking about human resources policies as investments. You ought to do cost analyses of turnover and mishiring, however. You might be even more startled about the size of those costs.

When we did our assessment program at Ford, we were given the cost figures for replacing a foreman or forewoman; at that time, Ford estimated it to be $50,000. I have been told that back in the 1970s insurance companies estimated the cost of replacing a life insurance sales representative to be $20,000. I spoke to an audience of pharmaceuticals sales managers in 1978 and asked them to estimate what it cost to replace a sales representative. Voices from the audience called out a range of figures: The average was about $25,000. What would a careful cost analysis show today?

If a new selection technology could enable you to reduce your hiring or promotion errors by only 10 percent—a modest gain, it would seem—you could afford to invest very large sums in such a new technology and still provide a considerable return on this investment to the company. In the end, of course, the managerial mind at the top has to visualize people both in human terms—as individuals to whom selection errors are extremely painful—and in economic terms—as an investment of the greatest consequence and not merely a new cost.

Appendix:
Five Case Studies

The following abstracts report the factual findings on the validity of track records when used to select or appraise key personnel. They are not intended to constitute complete research reports. Even if they did, the reader is cautioned that every company must revalidate any selection procedure to fit its own requirements and "culture."

Abstract	Topic
A	Selecting managers for profit objectives
B	Identifying the high-performing supervisor
C	Economic value of interpersonal competence
D	Concurrent validation in selecting for promotion in a state agency
E	Validity of critical incidents in the assessment and training of managerial judgment

Abstract A

Selecting Managers for Profit Objectives

Twenty-seven general plant managers were appraised with a TRI (Track Record Interview) and followed up five years later. How valid was the TRI system as an indicator of future management performance? It was found that the system successfully identified:

- 8 of the 10 general managers with the most profitable records over the next five years.

- 11 of the 17 general managers with the least profitable records over that period.

This is a hit rate of 70 percent. What does it mean in dollar terms?

The corporation manufactured and distributed food products in all 50 states. In sales, it was approximately 326 on the *Fortune*-500 list of the largest U.S. firms. Its major product division had 22 plants. A further analysis of the data for these 22 general managers was made, focusing on one aspect of the evaluation—their interpersonal competence.

The smaller division, with five plants, produced a different product. The interpersonal requirements for success in this division were not considered comparable to those in the larger division. Since N = 5 would not constitute a minimum statistical sample, the division was not included in the subsequent analysis.

Analysis of the 22 plants in the larger division showed that if, at the outset of the period, the corporation had retained only those managers with favorable interpersonal competence evaluations, it would have realized a net profit gain of $1,470,000 (in present dollars) for each of the following five years. This represents a profit gain from the TRI appraisal of $66,816 per manager for the first year (again in present dollars). Thus the first-year payback would have been about 55 to 1 over the cost of the TRI assessment.

It is doubtful that many chief executives would dispute the importance of interpersonal competence in a general manager. However, very few are aware of the enormous potential payback to be derived from using objective assessment to help make managerial promotion decisions, and of the less dramatic (but still definite) payback to be gained from using it to identify candidates for first-line supervision.

Abstract B

Identifying the High-Performing Supervisor

At Interstate Brands Corporation, a question arose as to whether the personnel department could help the sales department select good supervisors. To resolve this issue, 16 cases (each consisting of track record data collected from present supervisors, pulled from the files from the day they were hired) were used in the following experiment.

Five employment managers were asked to evaluate the data and to estimate the performance of the 16 supervisors. The sales supervisors' actual performance had been previously rated by the Eastern Division and Western Division sales managers (two echelons up from the supervisors). These ratings were on a 4-point scale, from 1 ("outstanding") to 4 ("not acceptable").

The employment managers did not know the identities of the 16 cases. Their ratings were then correlated with that of the division sales managers. The correlation was found to be .54.

The next question was: "Can other people be trained to evaluate supervisors in the same manner?"

Eight of the 16 cases (reflecting the entire range of rating categories) were used in a second experiment. Thirty-three personnel administrators, sales executives, and others enrolled in an MBA program were instructed in the track record concept and in the nature of the work of the sales supervisor at Interstate Brands. These 33 raters reviewed each of the eight cases and rated the supervisor's chances on the 4-point scale.

The findings were, again, a good match with the original division sales managers' ratings:

- Of the 229 ratings made by the 33 subjects, 43 were 1-ratings ("outstanding"); 34 of these ratings were correct. This is an efficiency rate of 79 percent.
- The subjects gave 34 4-ratings; 18 of these were correct. This is an efficiency rate of 53 percent.
- For all 229 ratings, the efficiency index was 70 percent. The chi-square measure of association was 98 (with 9 degrees of freedom)—a close and highly significant association.

The validity of the TR data is high in these experiments only because (1) the superiors rated the sales supervisors carefully, using an explicit job model; (2) the job model described behavior and results expected (not traits); (3) the job model was available as a frame of reference to guide the raters in both experiments.

Abstract C

Economic Value of Interpersonal Competence

This project attempted to determine whether certain interpersonal behavior patterns have a measurable effect on sales. One hundred sales representatives (from a computer-manufacturing firm with divisions in five countries) were interrogated to obtain recent critical sales incidents. These incidents were defined as episodes which demonstrated a very effective or ineffective relationship with a customer. About 250 such episodes were obtained and were confirmed by other observers as critical incidents.

Prior to the survey, 34 behaviors were identified as expected of all sales personnel in dealing with customers. The incidents were coded for the presence or absence of each of these behaviors. The tabulations were punchcarded and a computer analysis was then made to determine the degree of correlation between each trait and the outcome of the incidents. The most important outcomes correlated were whether a sale was made and how large it was. A high correlation would indicate behavior that helped make a sale or increase revenue.

Six behaviors were identified as having an especially large dollar value. This value was defined as the difference between the dollar outcome when the behavior was shown versus the dollar outcome when it was not shown. In other words, did the behavior make a difference? The values ranged from $90,000 to over $200,000. That is, a sales rep showing a particular behavior was producing that much more in sales than a rep who was not.

Verbatim examples of such behavior cannot be given, since this project report is the property of the manufacturing firm. However, the following disguised and abbreviated example is not atypical.

An American sales representative in France was approached by a government official unofficially and told that within 12 months the political climate would permit a "Buy American" option. Therefore, early preparation was advisable. The sales representative organized a team to conduct an ongoing investigation of the French government's potential needs for his company's new product line and succeeded in obtaining "sole source" opportunities to present the new line. When policy did change, the sales rep's division obtained orders totaling $6,000,000 before competing companies had positioned themselves even to make a proposal.

Statistically, these behaviors were all associated with dollar sales at levels of significance ranging from .001 to .0001 (that is, there was from one chance in a thousand to one chance in ten thousand that each finding could be due to random factors).

We recommended that sales reps be hired for and trained for these patterns. We also suggested that the dollar values of the behavior were so large that the selection and training designs would be worth extensive investment.

Abstract D
Concurrent Validation in Selecting for Promotion in a State Agency

The track records of 57 candidates for promotion to middle and top management in a major state agency were evaluated. A job model was constructed by the director and his two deputy directors for each of the two positions to be filled: supervisor and manager. Ten major goals were established for each position.

The assessment was entirely in written form. Each candidate was instructed in how to prepare the critical incidents and other track record documents to be used. A critical incident was prepared to show the candidate's past accomplishments with respect to each of the ten major goals in whichever position the candidate was seeking. The ten incidents were scored by an outside panel which had been trained to code critical incidents until agreement levels of 90 percent were attained. Three judges scored each critical incident. The total score for a candidate was the combination of their judgments of the frequency with which the candidate offered evidence for past attainment of each goal in the job model.

Each candidate prepared an annual report of success and failure for each of the last three years. These were scored as follows:

- Successes were credited if tangible evidence was offered.
- Failures were not subtracted but were considered as one type of evidence of candor.

The total score of the annual reports was the degree to which objective, verifiable results were reported for each of the three years. In brief, the candidate was credited for thinking about his or her work in an MBO (management by objectives) manner.

Finally, each candidate prepared an objective biographical inventory consisting of past accomplishments in a variety of work areas.

The annual reports were verified by interrogating the candidate's boss for the year covered by the report. The boss was not shown the report but instead was asked to volunteer the candidate's principal accomplishments for that year. The agreement was 88 percent on these facts. It did not prove necessary to discard any annual reports from the sample. This degree of credibility was due to the very narrow definition of "fact" that was used—for example, if a candidate claimed that he had opened up five new offices that year, meeting the agreed-on schedule, this was a fact that was relatively easy to verify in the interrogation of the boss. (Had we attempted to verify the candidate's self-ratings of traits, the outcome would obviously have been far less satisfactory.)

In another phase of the agency's evaluation of candidates, panels of interviewers subjectively rated the candidates' fitness for promotion.

Findings. Total scores of the three historical documents (critical incidents, annual reports, and biographical inventory) were correlated, along with interviewer ratings. The most reliable score was that of the biographical inventory ($r = .85$). The least reliable was that of the annual reports ($r = .65$). The correlations between the four total scores (three documents and interviewer ratings) were in the .40s. The agreement between total scores of the three historical documents and the agency's subjective ranking was very high in the case of candidates who had worked in the home office. It was much less in the case of candidates from the field. The plausible interpretation is that the agency top management had had opportunity to observe those who had worked in the home office.

Afterword. The results of this project were rather strongly applauded by a Boston University study of innovation in government—and bitterly opposed by the Civil Service Commission, which holds hearings for employees who feel they should have had higher scores in the "examination." The commission is currently being phased out through legislative reform, but in the meantime implementation of the new system will be delayed.

Abstract E

Validity of Critical Incidents in the Assessment and Training of Managerial Judgment

In a series of experiments using managers from several corporations (Interstate Brands, IBM, and Control Data), the value of critical incidents was tested in the following manner.

Twelve programmed cases were used in each experiment following the method described in C. A. Dailey, *Assessment of Lives* (Jossey-Bass, 1971). In this method, the predictive validity of critical incidents is measured for a manager making decisions about a person's probable performance. The manager's accuracy is compared only in relative terms. That is, does the manager become more accurate as the amount of information (number of critical incidents known) increases?

In the experiment, a critical incident (hereafter called Event A) was reviewed by the manager trainee. The trainee was then given correct Event B (along with two disguised distractors) and asked which of the three events was most likely in the performance of the person of whom Event A was true. After the trainee made the forecast, the correct Event B was identified. Now the trainee knew two facts: A and B. With these in mind, the trainee was asked to make the same forecast about Event C. The trainee continued in this manner until completing all 15 forecasts in the case. Then he or she continued with the next case. (Usually 12 cases were completed in the experiment.) The accuracy scores were based on up to 180 separate forecasts per trainee.

Since a programmed case is always an authentic, verified case, the resulting accuracy scores indicate validity of managerial judgment. With this assumption, the following scores were computed for each trainee:

- Accuracy score with very little information about each case (some people are better at such intuitive judgment than others).
- Accuracy score with maximum information about each case (some people carefully review the evidence and build up an advanced degree of understanding).
- Accuracy score in the total case.
- Accuracy score in early cases in the series.
- Accuracy score in later cases in the series.

In another experiment, trainees were given both the programmed case and the task described in Abstract B—namely, to review the application blank data on eight candidates for sales supervisor whose performance had been rated by their immediate superior to see whether they could predict these ratings. Thus it was possible to determine whether the programmed case method measured the same kind of managerial judgment as that required in reviewing application blank data taken from personnel files.

Findings. The findings from this experiment are summarized below.

1. Accuracy scores measured in the ways defined above have sufficient reliability for further research ("split half" $r = .75$ for the total cases). There is such an ability as predictive accuracy among managers.

2. For most managers, there is a sharp rise from the initial accuracy score (little information) to the maximum score. The shape of this learning curve is steep at the outset and then tapers off toward the end of the case.

3. For some, there is a more modest increase in validity from one case to the next.

4. When the trainees using the critical incidents described above were given a separate task (forecasting the performance ratings of sales supervisors—as in Abstract B), there was a correlation of .45 between the two accuracy scores.

5. People with experience in personnel management (including line managers who had hired personnel) performed better than those without experience.

Bibliography

Carlson, R. E., "The Relative Influence of Appearance and Factual Written Information on an Interviewer's Final Rating," *Journal of Applied Psychology* 51 (1967): 461–68.

Carlson, R. E., "Selection Interview Decisions: The Effect of Interviewer Experience, Relative Quota Situation, and Applicant Sample on Interviewer Decisions," *Personnel Psychology* 20 (1967): 259–80.

Dailey, Charles A., *Assessment of Lives*. San Francisco: Jossey-Bass, 1971.

Ghiselli, Edwin, *The Validity of Occupational Aptitude Tests*. New York: John Wiley & Sons, 1966.

Mayfield, E. C. "The Selection Interview: A Re-evaluation of Published Research," *Personnel Psychology* 17 (1964): 239–60.

Owens, William, "Background Data," in *Handbook of Industrial and Organizational Psychology*, edited by Marvin D. Dunnette. Chicago: Rand McNally, 1976.

Schmitt, Neal, "Social and Situational Determinants of Interview Decisions: Implications for the Employment Interview," *Personnel Psychology* 29 (1976): 79–101.

Springbett, B. M., "Factors Affecting the Final Decision in the Employment Interview," *Canadian Journal of Psychology* 12 (1958): 13–22.

Ulrich, L., and D. Trumbo, "The Selection Interview Since 1949," *Psychological Bulletin* 63 (1965): 100–116.

Wagner, R., "The Employment Interview: A Critical Summary," *Personnel Psychology* 2 (1949): 17–46.

Webster, E. C., *Decision-Making in the Employment Interview*. Montreal: Eagle, 1964.

Wernimont, Paul F., and John P. Campbell, "Signs, Samples, and Criteria," *Journal of Applied Psychology* 52 (1968): 372–76.

Wright, O. R., Jr., "Summary of Research on the Employment Interview Since 1964," *Personnel Psychology* 22 (1969): 391–413.

Index

DATE DUE

DEMCO 38-297